First World War
and Army of Occupation
War Diary
France, Belgium and Germany

2 DIVISION
Headquarters, Branches and Services
Commander Royal Artillery
1 December 1915 - 31 December 1915

WO95/1316/3

The Naval & Military Press Ltd
www.nmarchive.com
Published in association with The National Archives

Published by

The Naval & Military Press Ltd

Unit 10 Ridgewood Industrial Park,

Uckfield, East Sussex,

TN22 5QE England

Tel: +44 (0) 1825 749494

www.naval-military-press.com

www.nmarchive.com

This diary has been reprinted in facsimile from the original. Any imperfections are inevitably reproduced and the quality may fall short of modern type and cartographic standards.

© **Crown Copyright**
Images reproduced by permission of The National Archives, London, England, 2015.

Contents

Document type	Place/Title	Date From	Date To
Heading	2nd Div R.A., H.Q. War Diary December 1915		
War Diary	Bethune (47)	01/12/1915	31/12/1915
Miscellaneous	2nd Divisional Artillery Hostile Fire Report	01/12/1915	01/12/1915
Miscellaneous	R.A. 2nd Div	01/12/1915	01/12/1915
Miscellaneous	Action Time		
Miscellaneous	A Form Messages And Signals		
Miscellaneous	Daily Ammunition Return	01/12/1915	01/12/1915
Miscellaneous	2nd Divisional Artillery Orders By Brigadier-General G.H. Sanders, D.S.O., Comdg. R.A., 2nd Divn	01/12/1915	01/12/1915
Miscellaneous	2nd Divisional Artillery Hostile Fire Report 2nd December 1915	02/12/1915	02/12/1915
Miscellaneous	R.A. 2nd Divn	03/12/1915	03/12/1915
Miscellaneous	Diary	02/12/1915	02/12/1915
Miscellaneous	Action Time		
Miscellaneous	Daily Ammunition Return	02/12/1915	02/12/1915
Miscellaneous	2nd Divisional Artillery Orders By Brigadier-General G.H. Sanders, D.S.O., Comdg. R.A., 2nd Divn	02/12/1915	02/12/1915
Miscellaneous	2nd Divisional Artillery Hostile Fire Report	03/12/1915	03/12/1915
Miscellaneous	Action March		
Miscellaneous	R.A. 2 Div.	03/12/1915	03/12/1915
Miscellaneous	Daily Ammunition Return	03/12/1915	03/12/1915
Miscellaneous	2nd Divisional Artillery Orders By Brigadier-General G.H. Sanders, D.S.O., Comdg. R.A., 2nd Divn	03/12/1915	03/12/1915
Miscellaneous	2nd Divisional Artillery Hostile Fire Report	04/12/1915	04/12/1915
Miscellaneous	Z Group Diary	04/12/1915	04/12/1915
Miscellaneous	Group Diary	04/12/1915	04/12/1915
Miscellaneous	Daily Ammunition Return	04/12/1915	04/12/1915
Miscellaneous	R.A., 2nd Division Situation	04/12/1915	04/12/1915
Miscellaneous	G.O.C., R.A., 1st Corps	04/12/1915	04/12/1915
Miscellaneous	2nd Divisional Artillery Orders By Brigadier-General G.H. Sanders, D.S.O., Comdg. R.A. 2nd Divn	04/12/1915	04/12/1915
Miscellaneous	2nd Divisional Artillery Hostile Fire Report	05/12/1915	05/12/1915
Miscellaneous	Group Diary	05/12/1915	05/12/1915
Miscellaneous	Strong Point Destroyed This Week By 48th Batt	05/12/1915	05/12/1915
Miscellaneous	Z Group Diary	05/12/1915	05/12/1915
Miscellaneous	Daily Ammunition Return	05/12/1915	05/12/1915
Miscellaneous	A Form Messages And Signals		
Miscellaneous	2nd Divisional No: G.S. 778	05/12/1915	05/12/1915
Miscellaneous	2nd Division No: G.S. 778	05/12/1915	05/12/1915
Miscellaneous	2nd Division No: G.S. 744/2	05/12/1915	05/12/1915
Miscellaneous	A Form Messages And Signals		
Miscellaneous	2nd Divisional Artillery Orders By Brigadier-General G.H. Sanders, D.S.O., Comdg. R.A., 2nd Divn.	05/12/1915	05/12/1915
Miscellaneous	Group Diary	06/12/1915	06/12/1915
Miscellaneous	Z Group Diary	06/12/1915	06/12/1915
Miscellaneous	2nd Divisional Artillery Hostile Fire Report	06/12/1915	06/12/1915
Miscellaneous	Daily Ammunition Return	06/12/1915	06/12/1915
Miscellaneous	RA 2nd Divn.	07/12/1915	07/12/1915
Miscellaneous	2nd Divisional Artillery Orders By Brigadier-General G.H. Sanders, D.S.O., Comdg. R.A., 2nd Divn	06/12/1915	06/12/1915

Miscellaneous	2 Div. RA Diary	07/12/1915	07/12/1915
Miscellaneous	Action Time		
Miscellaneous	2nd Divisional Artillery Hostile Fire Report	07/12/1915	07/12/1915
Miscellaneous	Daily Ammunition Return	07/12/1915	07/12/1915
Miscellaneous	A Form Messages And Signals		
Miscellaneous	2nd Divisional Artillery Orders By Brigadier-General G.H. Sanders, D.S.O., Comdg R.A., 2nd Divn.	07/12/1915	07/12/1915
Miscellaneous	2 Div. R.A. Diary	08/12/1915	08/12/1915
Miscellaneous	Action Table		
Miscellaneous	2nd Divisional Artillery Hostile Fire Report	08/12/1915	08/12/1915
Miscellaneous	Daily Ammunition Return	08/12/1915	08/12/1915
Operation(al) Order(s)	2nd Division Artillery Operation Order No.9	08/12/1915	08/12/1915
Miscellaneous			
Miscellaneous	2nd Divisional Artillery Orders By Brigadier-General G.H. Sanders, D.S.O., Comdg. R.A., 2nd Division	08/12/1915	08/12/1915
Miscellaneous	A Form Messages And Signals		
Miscellaneous	2nd Div. RA Diary	09/12/1915	09/12/1915
Miscellaneous	Action Time		
Miscellaneous	2nd Divisional Artillery Hostile Fire Report	09/12/1915	09/12/1915
Miscellaneous	Daily Ammunition Return		
Miscellaneous	A Form Messages And Signals		
Miscellaneous	2nd Divisional Artillery Orders By Brigadier-General G.H. Sanders, D.S.O., Comdg. R.A. 2nd Divn	09/12/1915	09/12/1915
Miscellaneous	2nd Div. R.A. Diary	10/12/1915	10/12/1915
Miscellaneous	Principle Action		
Miscellaneous	2nd Divisional Artillery Hostile Fire Report	10/12/1915	10/12/1915
Miscellaneous	Daily Ammunition Return	10/12/1915	10/12/1915
Miscellaneous	Extract from Progress Report of 1st Battalion Herts. Regt.	05/12/1915	05/12/1915
Miscellaneous	2nd Divisional Artillery Orders By Brigadier-General G.H. Sanders, D.S.O., Comdg. R.A., 2nd Divn	10/12/1915	10/12/1915
Miscellaneous	R.A. 2 Div Diary	11/12/1915	11/12/1915
Miscellaneous	Action Time		
Miscellaneous	2nd Divisional Artillery Hostile Fire Report	11/12/1915	11/12/1915
Miscellaneous	A Form Messages And Signals		
Miscellaneous	Daily Ammunition Return	11/12/1915	11/12/1915
Miscellaneous	2nd Divisional Artillery Orders By Brigadier-General G.H. Sanders, D.S.O., Comdg. R.A., 2nd Divn	11/12/1915	11/12/1915
Miscellaneous	2nd Div. R.A.	12/12/1915	12/12/1915
Miscellaneous	Principle Action		
Miscellaneous	Group Diary	12/12/1915	12/12/1915
Miscellaneous	Z Group Diary	12/12/1915	12/12/1915
Miscellaneous	2nd Divisional Artillery Hostile Fire Report	12/12/1915	12/12/1915
Miscellaneous	Daily Ammunition Return	12/12/1915	12/12/1915
Miscellaneous	1st Corps Defence Scheme-Artillery	12/12/1915	12/12/1915
Miscellaneous	Southern Division Village Line		
Miscellaneous	Southern Division Le Touret Line		
Diagram etc	Diagram		
Miscellaneous	R.A., 2nd Division Situation	12/12/1915	12/12/1915
Miscellaneous	2nd Divisional Artillery Orders By Brigadier-General G.H. Sanders, D.S.O., Comdg. R.A., 2nd Divn.	12/12/1915	12/12/1915
Miscellaneous	RA 2nd Divn	13/12/1915	13/12/1915
Miscellaneous	Action Time		
Miscellaneous	Diary	13/12/1915	13/12/1915
Miscellaneous	Action Time		
Miscellaneous	Z Group Diary	13/12/1915	13/12/1915

Miscellaneous	Action Time		
Miscellaneous	2nd Divisional Artillery Hostile Fire Report	13/12/1915	13/12/1915
Miscellaneous	Daily Ammunition Return	13/12/1915	13/12/1915
Miscellaneous	2nd Divisional Artillery Orders By Brigadier-General G.H. Sanders, D.S.O., Comdg. R.A., 2nd Divn.	13/12/1915	13/12/1915
Miscellaneous	2nd Div Diary		
Miscellaneous	Action Time		
Miscellaneous	Diary	14/12/1915	14/12/1915
Miscellaneous	Action		
Miscellaneous	Diary Z Group	14/12/1915	14/12/1915
Miscellaneous	2nd Divisional Artillery Hostile Fire Report	14/12/1915	14/12/1915
Miscellaneous	Daily Ammunition Return		
Operation(al) Order(s)	2nd Divisional Artillery Operation Order No.10	14/12/1915	14/12/1915
Miscellaneous	Appendix A		
Miscellaneous	Appendix B		
Miscellaneous	2nd Divisional Artillery Orders By Brigadier-General G.H. Sanders D.S.O. Commanding R.A. 2nd Dn	15/12/1915	15/12/1915
Miscellaneous	Diary RA 2 Div	15/12/1915	15/12/1915
Miscellaneous	Action Time		
Miscellaneous	Diary	15/12/1915	15/12/1915
Miscellaneous	Action		
Miscellaneous	Diary	15/12/1915	15/12/1915
Miscellaneous	2nd Divisional Artillery Hostile Fire Report	15/12/1915	15/12/1915
Miscellaneous	Daily Ammunition Return	15/12/1915	15/12/1915
Miscellaneous	Wirecutting by 2nd Div Artillery	15/12/1915	15/12/1915
Miscellaneous	A Form Messages And Signals		
Miscellaneous	R.A. 2 Div	16/12/1915	16/12/1915
Miscellaneous	Action		
Miscellaneous	Diary	16/12/1915	16/12/1915
Miscellaneous	Action		
Miscellaneous	Z Group Diary	16/12/1915	16/12/1915
Miscellaneous	2nd Divisional Artillery Hostile Fire Report	16/12/1915	16/12/1915
Miscellaneous	Daily Ammunition Return	16/12/1915	16/12/1915
Miscellaneous	2nd Div RA Diary	17/12/1915	17/12/1915
Miscellaneous	Action		
Miscellaneous	2nd Divisional Artillery Hostile Fire Report	17/12/1915	17/12/1915
Miscellaneous	Daily Ammunition Return	17/12/1915	17/12/1915
Miscellaneous	2nd Divisional Artillery Orders By Brigadier-General G.H. Sanders, D.S.O., Comdg. R.A., 2nd Divn.	17/12/1915	17/12/1915
Miscellaneous	Diary 2nd Div RA	18/12/1915	18/12/1915
Miscellaneous	Action		
Miscellaneous	2nd Divisional Artillery Hostile Fire Report	18/12/1915	18/12/1915
Miscellaneous	Daily Ammunition Return	18/12/1915	18/12/1915
Miscellaneous	2nd Divisional Artillery Orders By Brig-General G.H. Sanders, D.S.O., C.R.A. 2nd Division	18/12/1915	18/12/1915
Miscellaneous	Diary RA 2nd Div	19/12/1915	19/12/1915
Miscellaneous	Action		
Miscellaneous	Diary		
Miscellaneous	Action		
Miscellaneous	Diary	19/12/1915	19/12/1915
Miscellaneous	2nd Divisional Artillery Hostile Fire Report	19/12/1915	19/12/1915
Miscellaneous	Daily Ammunition Return		
Miscellaneous	2nd Divisional Artillery Orders By Brigadier-General G.H. Sanders, D.S.O., Comdg. R.A., 2nd Divn	19/12/1915	19/12/1915
Miscellaneous	Diary RA 2nd Div	20/12/1915	20/12/1915
Miscellaneous	Action		

Miscellaneous	Diary Z Group	20/12/1915	20/12/1915
Miscellaneous	Action		
Miscellaneous	Diary	20/12/1915	20/12/1915
Miscellaneous	2nd Divisional Artillery Hostile Fire Report	20/12/1915	20/12/1915
Miscellaneous	Daily Ammunition Return	20/12/1915	20/12/1915
Miscellaneous	2nd Divisional Artillery Orders By Brigadier-General G.H. Sanders, D.S.O., Comdg. R.A., 2nd Division	20/12/1915	20/12/1915
Miscellaneous	Diary	21/12/1915	21/12/1915
Miscellaneous	Action		
Miscellaneous	Daily Diary Z Group Date 21.12.15	21/12/1915	21/12/1915
Miscellaneous	Action		
Miscellaneous	2nd Divisional Artillery Hostile Fire Report	21/12/1915	21/12/1915
Miscellaneous	Daily Ammunition Return	21/12/1915	21/12/1915
Miscellaneous	Diary	22/12/1915	22/12/1915
Miscellaneous	Action		
Miscellaneous	Diary	22/12/1915	22/12/1915
Miscellaneous	Action		
Miscellaneous	2nd Divisional Artillery Hostile Fire Report	22/12/1915	22/12/1915
Miscellaneous	Daily Ammunition Return	22/12/1915	22/12/1915
Operation(al) Order(s)	2nd Divisional Artillery Operation Order No.11	22/12/1915	22/12/1915
Miscellaneous	Report on Gas attack on night 21-22	22/12/1915	22/12/1915
Miscellaneous	Report On Night Operation	22/12/1915	22/12/1915
Miscellaneous	Operation On Z Front Night Of 21/22 Dec 1915		
Miscellaneous	Diary	23/12/1915	23/12/1915
Miscellaneous	Action		
Miscellaneous	Z Diary	23/12/1915	23/12/1915
Miscellaneous	Action		
Miscellaneous	2nd Divisional Artillery Hostile Fire Report	23/12/1915	23/12/1915
Miscellaneous	Daily Ammunition Return	23/12/1915	23/12/1915
Miscellaneous	A Form Messages And Signals		
Miscellaneous	2nd Divisional Artillery Orders By Brigadier-General G.H. Sanders, D.S.O., Comdg. R.A., 2nd Division	23/12/1915	23/12/1915
Miscellaneous	Diary	24/12/1915	24/12/1915
Miscellaneous	Action		
Miscellaneous	Z Diary	24/12/1915	24/12/1915
Miscellaneous	Action		
Miscellaneous	A Form Messages And Signals		
Miscellaneous	2nd Divisional Artillery Hostile Fire Report	24/12/1915	24/12/1915
Miscellaneous	Daily Ammunition Return	24/12/1915	24/12/1915
Miscellaneous	2nd Divisional Artillery Orders By Brigadier-General G.H. Sanders, D.S.O., Comdg. R.A., 2nd Divn.	24/12/1915	24/12/1915
Miscellaneous	Z Diary	25/12/1915	25/12/1915
Miscellaneous	Action		
Miscellaneous	Diary	25/12/1915	25/12/1915
Miscellaneous	Action		
Miscellaneous	2nd Divisional Artillery Hostile Fire Report	25/12/1915	25/12/1915
Miscellaneous	Daily Ammunition Return	25/12/1915	25/12/1915
Miscellaneous	2nd Divisional Artillery Orders By Brigadier-General G.H. Sanders, D.S.O., Comdg. R.A., 2nd Divn.	25/12/1915	25/12/1915
Miscellaneous	Diary	26/12/1915	26/12/1915
Miscellaneous	Action		
Miscellaneous	Daily Diary Date 26.12.15 Z Group RA	26/12/1915	26/12/1915
Miscellaneous	Action		
Miscellaneous	2nd Divisional Artillery Hostile Fire Report	26/12/1915	26/12/1915
Miscellaneous	Daily Ammunition Return	26/12/1915	26/12/1915

Miscellaneous	2nd Divisional Artillery Orders By Brigadier-General G.H. Sanders, D.S.O., Comdg. R.A., 2nd Divn.	26/12/1915	26/12/1915
Miscellaneous	Z Diary	27/12/1915	27/12/1915
Miscellaneous	Action		
Miscellaneous	Diary	27/12/1915	27/12/1915
Miscellaneous	Action		
Miscellaneous	2nd Divisional Artillery Hostile Fire Report	27/12/1915	27/12/1915
Miscellaneous	Daily Ammunition Return	29/12/1915	29/12/1915
Miscellaneous	2nd Divisional Artillery Orders By Brigadier-General G.H. Sanders, D.S.O., Comdg. R.A., 2nd Divn.	27/12/1915	27/12/1915
Miscellaneous	Z Diary	28/12/1915	28/12/1915
Miscellaneous	Action		
Miscellaneous	Diary	28/12/1915	28/12/1915
Miscellaneous	Action		
Miscellaneous	2nd Divisional Artillery Hostile Fire Report	28/12/1915	28/12/1915
Miscellaneous	Daily Ammunition Return	28/12/1915	28/12/1915
Miscellaneous	2nd Divisional Artillery Orders By Brigadier-General G.H. Sanders, D.S.O. Comdg. R.A. 2nd Division	28/12/1915	28/12/1915
Miscellaneous	Z Diary	29/12/1915	29/12/1915
Miscellaneous	Action		
Miscellaneous	Diary	29/12/1915	29/12/1915
Miscellaneous	Action		
Miscellaneous	2nd Divisional Artillery Hostile Fire Report	29/12/1915	29/12/1915
Miscellaneous	Daily Ammunition Return	29/12/1915	29/12/1915
Miscellaneous	2nd Divisional Artillery Orders By Brigadier-General G.H. Sanders, D.S.O., Comdg. R.A., 2nd Divn	29/12/1915	29/12/1915
Miscellaneous	Z Diary	30/12/1915	30/12/1915
Miscellaneous	Action		
Miscellaneous	Diary	30/12/1915	30/12/1915
Miscellaneous	Action		
Miscellaneous	2nd Divisional Artillery Hostile Fire Report	30/12/1915	30/12/1915
Miscellaneous	Daily Ammunition Return	30/12/1915	30/12/1915
Miscellaneous	2nd Divisional Artillery Orders By Brigadier-General G.H. Sanders, D.S.O., Comdg. R.A., 2nd Divn.	30/12/1915	30/12/1915
Miscellaneous	Z Group Diary	31/12/1915	31/12/1915
Miscellaneous	Action		
Miscellaneous	Diary A Group	31/12/1915	31/12/1915
Miscellaneous	Action		
Miscellaneous	Diary		
Miscellaneous	Action		
Miscellaneous	2nd Divisional Artillery Hostile Fire Report	31/12/1915	31/12/1915
Miscellaneous	Daily Ammunition Return	31/12/1915	31/12/1915

Index

SUBJECT.

No.	Contents.	Date.
	2ND DIV., R.A., H.Q. WAR DIARY, DECEMBER, 1915	

Army Form C. 2118.

WAR DIARY
or
INTELLIGENCE SUMMARY.
(Erase heading not required.)

Instructions regarding War Diaries and Intelligence Summaries are contained in F. S. Regs., Part II. and the Staff Manual respectively. Title pages will be prepared in manuscript.

Place	Date	Hour	Summary of Events and Information	Remarks and references to Appendices
BETHUNE (+7)	1. XII		Strong S. wind. Quiet day.	1537
			70th Battery to relieve 16th	1538
			Ammunition	1539
			Routine orders	1540
	2. XII		Generally quiet. Light fire - Batt. tired w. slight. We fired on Enemy	1541
			approx. 5-8 pm. Result unknown.	
			Ammunition	1542
			Routine orders	1543
	3. XII		Quiet day. Rain. Enemy in active	1544
			Ammunition	1545
			Routine orders	1546

WAR DIARY or INTELLIGENCE SUMMARY.

Army Form C. 2118.

Place	Date	Hour	Summary of Events and Information	Remarks and references to Appendices
	1915			
BETHUNE (4)	4.XII		Showery - Wind NW Strong - Enemy Quiet. No action of importance	1547
			Relief of 10th & 70th Completed	
			Ammunition	1548
			Weekly return of positions	1549
			Method of dealing with a Cuspula	1550
			Routine orders	1551
	5.XII		Fair light. Enemy more active than usual. Wind E to S 9mph.	1552
			Enemy caught moving in open in Subjenney. In action of importance	1553
			Ammunition	1554
			Report on ballistic cartridges lasting short in cord	1555
			Brens for withdrawal of 7 Mountain Battery	1556
			Training of East Anglian Div. Artillery	1557
			Brens for operation on 6th	1558
			Routine orders	1559

Army Form C. 2118.

WAR DIARY
or
INTELLIGENCE SUMMARY.
(Erase heading not required.)

Instructions regarding War Diaries and Intelligence Summaries are contained in F. S. Regs., Part II. and the Staff Manual respectively. Title pages will be prepared in manuscript.

Place	Date	Hour	Summary of Events and Information	Remarks and references to Appendices
BETHUNE (47)	1915 Dec 6 Monday		Fine day.	
			Firing of no importance on enemy communication trenches	1560
			Enemy showed no activity	1561
			Ammunition	1562
			Msg of fire	1563
			Routine Orders	1564
	Tuesday 7		Fine day. Wind S.W. Sunny.	
			No action of importance	1565
			Enemy showed some activity	1566
			Ammunition	1567
			Routine Orders	15-68

Army Form C. 2118.

WAR DIARY
or
INTELLIGENCE SUMMARY.
(Erase heading not required.)

Instructions regarding War Diaries and Intelligence Summaries are contained in F. S. Regs., Part II. and the Staff Manual respectively. Title pages will be prepared in manuscript.

Place	Date	Hour	Summary of Events and Information	Remarks and references to Appendices
BETHUNE (41)	1915 Dec. Wed. 8		Fine day - No important action Enemy shows no special activity Ammunition	1569 1570 1571
		7.15P	Operation order for 9th issued	1572
			Routine Orders	1573
	Thursday 9		Thick mist till. Weather of very importance - Operations abandoned Enemy is active Ammunition Night lines for 59th Inf. Bde. Routine orders	1574 1575 1576 1577 1578

Army Form C. 2118.

WAR DIARY
or
INTELLIGENCE SUMMARY.
(Erase heading not required.)

Instructions regarding War Diaries and Intelligence Summaries are contained in F. S. Regs., Part II. and the Staff Manual respectively. Title pages will be prepared in manuscript.

Place	Date	Hour	Summary of Events and Information	Remarks and references to Appendices
BETHUNE (F)	1915 Dec. Friday 10		Early fine, light good. Moderate wind.	1579
			Enemy caught running in several places.	1580
			No activity by enemy.	1581
			Ammunition.	
			Quick action by 15" Battery.	1582
			Routine orders.	1583
	Saturday 11		Fine day, light wind, limit for 27 wet.	1584
			No special action.	1585
			Enemy's action - some activity.	
			Report on Shelling Canton by 60 pdr.	1586
			Ammunition.	1587

Army Form C. 2118.

WAR DIARY
or
INTELLIGENCE SUMMARY.
(Erase heading not required.)

Instructions regarding War Diaries and Intelligence Summaries are contained in F.S. Regs, Part II. and the Staff Manual respectively. Title pages will be prepared in manuscript.

Place	Date	Hour	Summary of Events and Information	Remarks and references to Appendices
BETHUNE (4)	1915 Dec. Sunday 12		Very fine day. Am rain. Light N.9. wind & F.S. Work	
			We caught improvement in Sectoral places	1586
			Enemy inactive	1589
			Ammunition	1590
			Defence Scheme Submitted	1591
			Situation Return	1592
			Routine orders	1594
	Monday 13		Fair day — Light South moderate wind N.	1595
			No special activity. Own movement.	
			Enemy shows little activity	1596
			Ammunition	1597
			Routine orders	1598

Army Form C. 2118.

WAR DIARY
or
INTELLIGENCE SUMMARY.
(Erase heading not required.)

Instructions regarding War Diaries and Intelligence Summaries are contained in F. S. Regs., Part II. and the Staff Manual respectively. Title pages will be prepared in manuscript.

Place	Date	Hour	Summary of Events and Information	Remarks and references to Appendices
BETHUNE (41)	1915 Dec. Tuesday 14		Dull day. Wet. Wind S. 8mph.	
			No action of importance. Enemy taught moving in a few places	1599
			Enemy quiet	1600
			Ammunition	1601
		10.30 p	Operation Orders for 15th issued	1602
			Routine orders	1603
		Wednesday 15	Fine day. Wind S½E to SE moderate. Light frost.	
			Bombardment of Pietstack area carried out. Mich at. No other action of importance.	1604
			Enemy inactive	1605
			Ammunition	1606
			Report on wire cutting	1607
			Second phase of operations postponed	1608

Army Form C. 2118.

WAR DIARY
or
INTELLIGENCE SUMMARY.
(Erase heading not required.)

Instructions regarding War Diaries and Intelligence Summaries are contained in F. S. Regs., Part II. and the Staff Manual respectively. Title pages will be prepared in manuscript.

Place	Date	Hour	Summary of Events and Information	Remarks and references to Appendices
BETHUNE (47)	1915 Dec Thursday 16		Dull dark day. Was light. Mine S. Gorenate	
			Movement caught in one or two places	1609
			Enemy made an organized retaliation on our front	1610
			Ammunition	1611
	Friday 17		Dull day, misty. Rain.	
			Very quiet.	1612
			Enemy inactive generally, but put French supplement to 2	1613
			Ammunition	1614
			Routine Orders	1615
	Saturday 18		Thick misty day — all find ESE 5mh	
			Some fire in retaliation to enemy	1616
			Enemy took advantage of thick day	1617
			Ammunition	1618
			Routine Orders	1619

Army Form C. 2118.

WAR DIARY
or
INTELLIGENCE SUMMARY.
(Erase heading not required.)

Instructions regarding War Diaries and Intelligence Summaries are contained in F.S. Regs., Part II. and the Staff Manual respectively. Title pages will be prepared in manuscript.

Place	Date	Hour	Summary of Events and Information	Remarks and references to Appendices
BETHUNE (4.7)	1915 Dec 19 Sunday		Fine day. Much demonstration from Mts. 7 work done. Wind N.	
			Some activity, movement caught in a few places.	1620
			Little activity by enemy.	1621
			Ammunition	1622
			Routine orders	1623
	Dec 20 Monday		Thick misty day. Little doing.	1624
			Snowy, no	1625
			Place B of Operation order 10 no. to have come off but was failed.	
			Ammunition	1626
			Routine orders	1627
	21 Tuesday		Misty day. Light thaw. Little to be seen. Wind W. slight	
			A good deal of fire in retaliation	1628
			Enemy took advantage of thick day	1629
			Ammunition	1630
		s/s	See attack carried out according to programme - 60.10.	

Army Form C. 2118.

WAR DIARY
or
INTELLIGENCE SUMMARY.
(Erase heading not required.)

Instructions regarding War Diaries and Intelligence Summaries are contained in F. S. Regs., Part II. and the Staff Manual respectively. Title pages will be prepared in manuscript.

Place	Date	Hour	Summary of Events and Information	Remarks and references to Appendices
BETHUNE (17)	1915 December 22 Wed.		Fine day. All quiet. No action of importance - hm2 N. Slight Ammunition	1631
			Operation order 11 issued for night firing	1632
				1633
			Report on gas attack 9.21 P.	1634
	23 Thursday		Fine day. Light frost. hm2 Sir. vanilla but to strong	1635
			No action of importance beyond retaliation	1636
			Enemy fairly active	1637
			Ammunition	1638
			Operations by Renies on 21st	1639
			Routine Orders	
	24 Friday		Some rain all day. hm2 Sir. strong. No hostile 7.15 - 3.45. No action of importance except night firing as usual hyns, an] firing on TRIANGLE by heavies. Some shells fell short in talbot pm(annexure)	1640
				1641

T2134. Wt. W708—776. 500000. 4/15. Sir J. C. & S.

Army Form C. 2118.

WAR DIARY
or
INTELLIGENCE SUMMARY.
(Erase heading not required.)

Instructions regarding War Diaries and Intelligence Summaries are contained in F. S. Regs., Part II. and the Staff Manual respectively. Title pages will be prepared in manuscript.

Place	Date	Hour	Summary of Events and Information	Remarks and references to Appendices
BETHUNE (47)	1915 December 24 Friday		Report on enemy's action — little activity. Ammunition Expenditure Routine Ams	1642 1643 1644
	25 Saturday		Showery. Wind Sn. Smly. Slo horrible 7-4. Light good. Programme of night firing carried out with modifications. Enemy's action — slight. Ammunition Expenditure Routine Orders	1645 1646 1647 1648
	26 Sunday		Showery. Wind Sn. moderate. Slo hm. 7.30 — 7. Light fair to good. Fairly quiet all day. Enemy slightly more active. Ammunition Expenditure Routine Orders	1649 1650 1651 1652

WAR DIARY
or
INTELLIGENCE SUMMARY.

Army Form C. 2118.

Place	Date	Hour	Summary of Events and Information	Remarks and references to Appendices
BETHUNE (4)	1915 Dec. 27 Monday		Stormy S.W. wind. Obs. poor. 7.15 – 4. Light good. No special activity.	1653
			Enemy hit and partly wrecks the cone 140.	1654
			Ammunition Expenditure	1655
			Routine Orders	1656
	28 Tuesday		Wind S. Slight. Obs poor 7.15 - 4. Light good. Unusual ships shews by enemy and some activity in trenches.	1657
			Ammunition	1658
			Routine Orders	1659
	29 Wednesday		Misty, any wind SE to SSW moderate. Obs. poor the 7.30 – 4. Very quiet.	1660
			Ammunition	1661
			Routine Orders	1662

Army Form C. 2118.

WAR DIARY
or
INTELLIGENCE SUMMARY.
(Erase heading not required.)

Instructions regarding War Diaries and Intelligence Summaries are contained in F. S. Regs., Part II. and the Staff Manual respectively. Title pages will be prepared in manuscript.

Place	Date	Hour	Summary of Events and Information	Remarks and references to Appendices
BETHUNE (47)	1915 DEC 30 Thursday		Misty day. Obs. from 7.15 - 4. Light frost. Enemy blew up a mine in Y2 and some shelling followed. Ammunition Routine orders	1663 1664 1665
	31 Friday		Fine day. Obs from 7.15 - 3 pm. Light frost to good. Some little activity by enemy. Ammunition expenditure	1666 1667

2nd Divisional Artillery

HOSTILE FIRE REPORT.

1st December 1915.

1. GENERAL INFORMATION.

This evening, tower at WINGLES was on fire, the fire seemed to be spreading. Probably vaused by our shell fire.

Enemy sent up several green and white lights at 5-10 p.m. to-day when our artillery south of Z group opened fire on DUMP neighbourhood.

2 HOSTILE FIRE.

No.	Time. From	To	Nature	Direction From	Aera Shelled.	Remarks.
1	30th Nov. 6-30p	8-0p	77mm	-	The LANE WILSON'S WAY	
2	1st Decr. 8-10a	8-20a	77mm	AUCHY	SIM/S KEEP	
3	9-30a	-	-	-	ANNEQUIN	Enemy obtained 1 direct hit on a cooker. The cook was thrown some distance into the air and the dinner spoiled but no casualties at all
4	10-15a	10-35a	77mm	AUCHY	F 29 b 9.8	1 round every few mins
5	10-30a	10-35a	105mm	?	PONT FIXE	
6	11-0a	-	105mm	?	WESTMINSTER Br	
7	11-30a	12 noon	77mm	?	CUINCHY	
8	11-30a	,,	105cm	AUCHY	400 House	
9	12-30p	12-40p	77mm	-	A 21 d 1.5 trenches.	
10	3-15p	3-50p	77mm	?	HOLLOW	
11	5-15p	-	77mm & 105mm	LA BASSEE	SIDSURY SPOIL BANK	

A. Durand Lt.
for.

Major R.A.
Brigade Major R.A. 2nd Divn.

R.A. 2nd Div. DIARY.

DATE. 1. Dec. 1915

OBSERVATION CONDITIONS. Observation possible 7.15 am to 4 pm. Light very good all day. Wind S. 30 m.p.h.

WORK DONE BY ENEMY. Some digging has been done near N. exits of Auchy.

Two white flags and a tape seen about A 29 b 0.9 – 9.1, apparently trace for new trench. (Registered)

MOVEMENT SEEN.
Working parties seen – A 21 b 8.9 (12.17 pm) A 22 b 5.3.7.4 (9 am.) A 21 d 7.5 (2.15 pm) A 28 b 7.5 (3.15 pm)

GUNS LOCATED OR SUSPECTED.
A 17 d 9.9 seems a centre of artillery activity, 4.2 and 77 shells coming straight up the canal.

WORK DONE BY US.

GENERAL.
A certain amount of hostile artillery activity.
Metallurgique works near Wingles partly set on fire 4.30 pm.
Enemy sent up several green and white lights at 5.10 pm when our artillery 15th Divn. opened on Dump neighbourhood.
There is a small white flag put up on a tree N.q Lone Farm.

ACTION.   See Over.

J. Hunkers Major
~~Lt. Colonel~~
~~Commanding~~ B.R.A.

ACTION					
Time From	To	Battery	Target	Rounds	Remarks.
6p	10p	70	Main road by Auchy	18	to catch transport
6.30p	8p	9	2nd line trenches A1	25	retaliation
8p		15	Madagascar tr	10	by request
7.35a		17	trenches Z3	8	movement seen
8.30a		48	Mine P⁻	12	retaliation
9a	9.10	9	A22 b 5 3 - 7 4	40	working party
9.45a		17	trenches Z3	6	movement
10 a		48	Lean to Cottage	15	destruction
10 a	5pm	59S	various	52	registration
10.15	11a	50	Embankment rd & Barge Bridge	30	Retaliation
		56	do do	18	do
10.30		15	Les Briques	8	instruction
10.45		71	Canteleux	16	retaliation
10.50		17	Snipers Post	10	
11	11.30	48	Les Briques Railway Cottage	25	Destruction & registration
			Fore	28	Suspected O.P.
11.25		15	Auchy	18	Retaliation
11.43	12.13	47	Auchy	40	Suspected O.P. & retaliation
11.30a	1p	9	"	10	retaliation
12.20p		15	Madagascar	18	Flashes
1p	2p	71	A 17d	16	5 direct hits
2p	2.10	71	MG on TORTOISE		working party dispersed
2.15p		17	A 21d 7.5	77	Enfilading trenches
2.30p	3.30p	7 How	Brickstack area	10	Suspected OP
2p		48	House A 30 d 1 9	11	Registration
3.15		15	Brickstack A 16 C	15	trace of new trench regn?
3.15		17	A 29 b 0.9 - 9.1	13	trench mortar active
3.38		56	A Brickstack	5	working party
3.45	3.55	47	A 28 6 7.5	9	Cooking dug out
4		56	A 22 a 2.2		

"A" Form.
Army Form C. 2121.
MESSAGES AND SIGNALS. No. of Message............

Prefix ...... Code ...... m	Words	Charge	This message is on a/c of:	Recd. at 1536 m
Office of Origin and Service Instructions.	Sent			Date
	At ...... m		......Service.	From
	To			By
	By		(Signature of "Franking Officer.")	

TO { A Group 7" Bde
       3rd Bde. RFA

| Sender's Number. | Day of Month. | In reply to Number | AAA |
| BM G 39 | | | |

7th Battery will detach
16th on counter battery work
and will take over its position
and 16th will take over 70th
position and will be attached
to A Group own arrangements
to be made mutually between
brigade commanders concerned — report
will be made when 16th in 70th position —

From
Place R A 1 Div
Time 7.13 pm

Censor. _J. Mackay Major_
Signature of Addressor or person authorised to telegraph in his name.

* This line should be erased if not required.

1539

DAILY AMMUNITION RETURN

DATE 1st Decr 1915

BATTERIES.

Piece	Projectile	Code	50	70	15	48	71	9	16	17	47	56	Total	Per Piece
18-pr	Guns.......													
	Shrapnel...	"A"	28	20	79	171	8	214	140	13	–	–	673	
	H. E.......	"Ax"	14	19	–	35	61	178	1	53	–	–	361	
4.5"	Howitzers..													
	Shrapnel...	"B"									2	–	2	
	H. E.......	"Bx"									32	66	98	

2nd Divisional Artillery Orders.

by

Brigadier-General G.H.SANDERS, D.S.O., Comdg.R.A., 2nd Divn.

1st December,1915.

1148. R.A.ORDERS.

Were not issued yesterday, 30th November,1915.

1149. COURTMARTIAL.

A F.G.C.M. will assemble at Headquarters, R.A., 2nd Division (18 RUE SADI-CARNOT, BETHUNE) at 10-0 a.m. on Saturday, 4th December,1915, for the trial of No.35158 Dr. J. Howat, 44th B.A.C., and No.59717 Dr. J.Dyer, 71st Battery, R.F.A., and such other accused as may be brought before it:-

PRESIDENT.
Major C.D.G.Lyon. - 16th Battery, R.F.A.

MEMBERS.
Captain I.C.Pery Knox Gore. - 70th Battery, R.F.A.
Lieutenant E.G.Barkham. - 71st Battery, R.F.A.

The accused to be warned and all witnesses duly required to attend.
Proceedings to be forwarded to Staff Captain, R.A., 2nd Division.
Court Orderly to be supplied by 44th Brigade, R.F.A.

1150. RETURNS.

O's.C. units are reminded that Ammunition returns are due in this office at 12-30 p.m. daily.

1151. PROMOTION.

No.21515. B.Q.M.S. Farr, 15th Battery is confirmed in his rank with effect from 29-8-1915, vice "Diacon" to England.

1152. TRANSPORT - INDENTIFICATION MARK

The 2nd Division indentification marked issued today, will be painted on all transport vehicles.

1153. LEAVE.

New allotment for leave which is open again :-

Wednesday.	28 men.	44th Bde.	Sunday.	28 men.	34th Bde.
Thursday.	28 "	D.A.C.	Monday.	28 "	36th "
Friday.	15 "	36th Bde.	Tuesday.	28 "	41st "
	9 "	7th Mtn.Bty.			
	3 "	D.A.C.			
	2 "	Spare.			
Saturday	15 "	41st Bde.			
	7 "	34th "			
	5 "	44th "			
	1 "	D.A.C.			

A.DURAND, Lieut,R.A.,
a/Staff Captain, R.A., 2/Divn.

2nd Divisional Artillery

HOSTILE FIRE REPORT.   2nd December 1915.

No.	Time From	To	Nature	Direction From	Area Shelled.	Remarks.
1	9-0a	9-30a	77mm	-	A 15 a 6.4	A few rounds
2	10-5a	10-30a	4.2"	-	HOLLOW and BULGE	
3	10-5a	10-10a	77mm	-	A 21 b	Trenches
4	11-22a	11-30a	77mm	-	PONT FIXE	A few rounds
5	12-55p		77mm	-	A 21 d 1.5	
6	2-42p	2-50p	77mm	Straight down Canal	SIDBURY & PONT FIXE	
7	3-20p	3-30p	105mm	-	A 21 b	Trenches
8	3-25p	3-35p	77mm	Straight down Canal	PONT FIXE Distillery	8 rounds.

A. Durand
for Major R.A.
Brigade Major R.A. 2nd Div.

R.A. 2nd Div.   3.12.15

Yesterday
 Between 5 PM and 8 PM the
following points were fired at
at irregular intervals.

- 71st By. { PLAIN ALLEY.
  70 Rounds. { TRACK E OF CANTELEUX
              ALLEY S.

    at varying ranges.

- 50th Batty. { TOW PATH N & S of
  60 Rounds. { CANAL from A.16.b.8.8
              to A.17.d.2.9.

    at varying ranges.

- 56th How. By.   CANTELEUX.
  15 Rounds

- 59th Siege.   Work at A.17.a.6.7.
  12 Rounds.

The only retaliation provoked was
about 5.30 pm when 4 Pipsqueaks
were fired along CANAL near PONT
    FIXE.   H Ward Lt Col

Recd 10.25am 3/12/15

DIARY.

DATE 8/12/15

OBSERVATION CONDITIONS. Observation possible 7.20 am – 3.30 pm
Light medium all day –

WORK DONE BY ENEMY.
On trenches near Culvert at W. End of Triangle – loophole
for MG or observation clearly visible at A16a2.1
Enemy have put up a board on their front line opposite
A17a0.22. It is conjectured that this is to mark a point on the
same system as we use.
MOVEMENT SEEN. Work continued on W. exits of Auchy.
In A17a – Plain alley probably waterlogged –

GUNS LOCATED OR SUSPECTED.

nil

WORK DONE BY US.

—

GENERAL.
The Mound at A17a6.6 was attacked with 120 rounds HE
wood and Earth were thrown up, but no signs were seen of
Steel or Concrete. Enemy showed much interest, and at
close several appeared and inspected damage.
They were fired on with good results.
A Black dog ran out of the German lines in 22 at 2.55 pm
and ran back again –

ACTION.   See Over.
                                        Lt. Colonel.
                                      Commanding
                                        Burke

ACTION

Time From	To	Battery	Target	Rounds	Remarks
8.15p		15	Madagascar trench	6	harrassment
10.30p			" "	10	"
4 a			" "	8	"
11 a	11.25a		Auchy	95	Suspected O.P.
12			Lone Farm	8	instruction
4 p			Brickstacks	4	registration
10.45p	11 p	48	Auchy	12	
8.30a			Cooking behind Mine Pt	8	
9.15 a	9.45a		Auchy	50	Suspected OP
3 p	3.15p		Dock Alley	20	Instruction
3.15p			Hindenburg tr.	25	"
7.35a		17	Z2 point	8	Working party
9.18a			Lone Farm	10	
1.5p			Z2 point	15	instruction
3.30p			Z2 point work party	10	Black Dog dispersed
10 a	10.45a	47	Branch Keep	11	with air observation
11.55a	12.1p	9	A 29 b work party	8	dispersed
12.25p	12.45p		A 23 a ½ 5	25	Suspected O.P.
1.45p			A 23 c 0.8	15	"
95 p	2.20p		Auchy	20	retaliation
3 p			A 29 b work party	5	
9a		71	A 16 a 5.9	7	Retaliation
10 a			Railway trench	10	
10.30	11.30		A 17 a 6.6	103	Mound - destruction
11.15p			Fosse tr.	8	
2.45p			M.G. Emplacement	15	damaged
			Madagascar tr.	19	instruction
9.30	3.30	H.V.	Brickstacks	70	Enfilade
12	1		Map Pt	35	
5p		59 Hoy	A 17 a 6.7	4	Registration
6.20p		70	A Brickstack	3	M.G.
11.10a			A 16 d 2.1	6	Work party
2 p			A x 6 8.7½	9	M.G. firing on aeroplane
11 a	12	50	Mound A 17 a 6.6	20	
3.30p			Ho. A 16 d 8½.3	12	Retaliation
9.45a		56	A 16 a 2.1	12	Loophole
11.10a			A 17 a 6.7	5	Movement
2.20p			Cantelemot	10	House

DAILY AMMUNITION RETURN

DATE 2nd Decr 1915

BATTERIES.

Piece	Projectile	Code	50	70	15	48	71	9	16	17	47	56	Total Per Piece
18-pr	Guns......												
	Shrapnel...	"A"	39	19	80	115	5	13	81	29	-	-	381
	H. E......	"Ax"	16	7	3	15	123	44	-	12	-	-	220
4.5"	Howitzers..												
	Shrapnel...	"B"									-	-	-
	H. E......	"Bx"									21	39	60

2nd Divisional Artillery Orders

by

Brigadier-General G.H.SANDERS, D.S.O., Comdg.R.A., 2nd Divn.

2nd December, 1915.

1154. CHILLED FEET and FROSTBITE - PREVENTION OF.

Particular attention is directed to paragraph 1275 of General Routine Orders, dated 28th November, 1915. The instructions contained therein should be communicated to all ranks as early as possible. Units will report to this Headquarters when this has been done.

A.DURAND, Lieut, R.A.

a/Staff Captain, R.A., 2nd Divn.

2nd Divisional Artillery

HOSTILE FIRE REPORT.

3rd December, 1915.

No.	Time From	To	Nature	Direction From	Aera Shelled	Remarks
	2nd Decr.					
1.	7-30p	7-35p	77mm	?	HARLEY St.	30 rounds
	3rd Decr.					
2.	12-30p	1-0p	77mm	LA BASSEE	GIVENCHY	
3.	2-0p	2-30p	77mm	,,	GUNNER Siding	
4.	2-3p	2-18p	77mm	HAISNES	Z2	25 rounds
5.	2-20p	2-30p	77mm	,,	CAMBRIN	4 ,,
6.	2-45p		4.2"	?	A 19 d 5.6	2; 1 air, 1 per.
7.	3-0p		77mm	?	MOUNTAIN He	
8.	3-10p	3-30p	77mm	AUCHY ?	PONT FIXE	
9.	3-45p	3-50p	77mm	?	PUDDING Lane	6 rounds
10.	4-5p	4-10p	77mm	HAISNES or AUCHY	TOURBIERES and road	12 rounds in groups of 4 at 1 second interval.

A Durand
for Major R.A.
Brigade Major R.A. 2nd Divn.

ACTION Time From	To	Battery	Target	Rounds	Remarks
5.10 p		15	Auchy	15	Retaliation
9.30 a	2.15 p		Madagascar tr. and new trenches A28	42	"
2.30 p			Haisnes	7	"
3 p			new trenches	2	"
3.10			Extaminet A29a	19	Instruction
12.45 p		48	des Briques	12	Instruction
2.10 p			Mine Pt. Mine alley	30	retaliation for Minnie
3.30			Auchy A23C27	10	retaliation
4.10			A23C46		
			Mine Pt	4	"
9 p		9	Trenches by ETNA	4	by request
10 p	3 a.m.		Trenches	8	
1 pm			A1 trenches	8	retaliation for Minnie
2.40 p			A17C5.2	10	retaliation for field gun - ceased
11.55 p		47	Ryan Keep	4	By request
10.40 a			Franks Keep	2	
12.50 p			Ryan Keep	4	retaliation for Minnie
3 p		59 Siege	A30 C9 4	2	registration
12.15 p		50	Mound A17a7.7	18	testing fuzes
5 p	8 p		Towpath A16d8.8 to A17d29 both banks	60	
3 p	3.15 p	"	Embankment R̄ & N.E. Brickstack	17	retaliation
5 p	8 p	70	Plain Alley Track E & Canteleux alley S	70	varying ranges
	7 p		Canteleux	10	
	7 p	2.20 p	A17a7.7 A16a28	20	retaliation
5 p	8 p	56	Canteleux	40	
8.45 p			Minenwerfer	8	by request (suspd)
12.15 p	12.30 p	7 How	Behind brickstacks	22	
2.30 p	3.15 p		Triangle	38	
5 p	8 p	59 Siege	Work A17a6.7	12	

R.A. 7 Div. DIARY.

DATE 3/12/15

OBSERVATION CONDITIONS. Observation possible 12.30 to 3.30 p.m., poor. Rain most of day. Wind E by S. 9 m.h.

WORK DONE BY ENEMY.
LEAN TO COTTAGE has entirely disappeared, the remains having apparently been removed.
No fresh work seen.

MOVEMENT SEEN.
When mist cleared some Germans seen moving towards at house A 30 d 1.5

GUNS LOCATED OR SUSPECTED.
nil

WORK DONE BY US.
nil

GENERAL.
70th Battery has relieved 16th for counter battery work.
From 5 to 8 p.m. (2nd) we directed intermittent fire against communications in B1. The enemy did not retaliate.

ACTION.   See Over.

A. Mowbray Major
18th R.A.
Lt. Colonel.
Commanding

DAILY AMMUNITION RETURN

DATE 3rd Decr '15

BATTERIES.

Piece	Projectile	Code	50	70	15	48	71	9	16	17	47	56	Total Per Piece
18-pr	Guns.......												
	Shrapnel...	"A"	86	4	26	41	4	41	44	74	-	-	353
	H. E.	"Ax"	-	17	-	30	72	210	-	23	-	-	352
4.5"	Howitzers..												
	Shrapnel...	"B"									-	-	-
	H. E.	"Bx"									6	54	60

1546

2nd Divisional Artillery Orders

by

Brigadier-General G.H.SANDERS, D.S.O., Comdg.R.A., 2nd Divn.

3rd December, 1915.

1155. GUM BOOTS.

The report called for in 2nd Division No.3344/8 will be rendered to this office by noon on Sunday, 5th December,15.

1156. WATER-TROUGHS.

All units who have not yet made water-troughs for their wagon lines should do so without delay.
The authority for drawing the necessary material from the C.R.E., will be obtained from this office.

1157. COURTMARTIAL.

No.26526, Dr. J.Dixon, 2nd Division Ammunition Column, attached H.Q., 2nd Division will be tried by the F.G.C.M. ordered to assemble to-morrow, Saturday, 4th instant.

A.DURAND, Lieut, R.A.
a/Staff Captain, R.A., 2nd Divn.

N O T I C E.

LOST - On Thursday evening between Beuvry and Cambrin, heavily built grey mare, carrying officer's saddle and snaffle bridle. If found please communicate with O.C., 44th Brigade Ammunition Column.

2nd Divisional Artillery

HOSTILE   FIRE   REPORT.

4th December, 1915.

No.	Time From	Time To	Nature.	Direction from	Area shelled.	Remarks
1	9-0a	2-0p	77mm	CANTELEUX	SIDBURY	Intermittent
2	9-35a	9-40a	77mm	?	56 gun position	A 20 a 4.0
3	11-25a		,,	A 18 a 1.1		
4	12-10p	12-25p	,,	AUCHY	Trench A 27b	12 rounds 48th Retaliated
5	12-45p		,,	?	Trench A 21a	3 rounds
6	1-25p	1-50p	10 cm	?	Trench A 27c	20 rounds
7	1-35p	2-0p	105mm	?	CUINCHY & COWL House	6 rounds
8	2-30p		77mm	AUCHY or HAISNES	A 19 d 5.6	4 rounds (2 air) The range appeared long and the shell tired.

A.Durand
for Major R.A.
Brigade Major R.A. 2nd Divn.

Z GROUP DIARY.

B.

DATE - 4-12-15.

General. Signalling was again seen in DOUVRIN but nothing could be read. 15 min left of Douvrin church.

Fire at 'MELLALURGIQUE' works has destroyed the foot of the tower and the scaffolding.

[Enemy's Works. nothing to report.]

Light at intervals during morning good. Two germans were seen near house A 30 d 0.5. 17th Batt killed one german near A 29 a 45.55 he was seen to fall and wriggle. This party was in the open when the mist cleared.

Action.

No.	Time. From.	To.	Battery.	Target.	Rounds.	Remarks.
1	2 pm		9th Batt	Mill Alley	8	working party
2	2.30 pm			Auchy A 22 b 5.6	5	suspected M.G. retaliation.
3	5.45 pm	6 pm	15th Batt	Madagascar	29	by request
4	12 mid	12.10 pm		"	28	"
5	11 am			Front line generally	9	"
6	12.10 pm			New trenches	29	retaliation
7	1 pm			Madagascar	12	"
8	10 am		17th Batt	Lone farm	4	working party
9	10.10 am			A 29 a 45.55 party.	2	1 killed
10	2.35 pm			A 29 b 5.1	7	retaliation
11	2.55 pm			front to.	16	working party

Lieut. Colonel.
Commanding   Group.

12	3.55pm		17th Batt	SNIPERS post	1 rd	
13	4.38pm 3rd 12-15		47th	AUCHY A23 b 9.3	8	retaliation
14	10.42am			Bushes in Connection q A29 a 95.25		registration

15	9pm	10pm	48th	Front & support tr	80	by request in retaliation
16	11pm			Auchy	9	
17	7am		71st X and 48th	{ Haines { Auchy	21	
18	12 noon		48th	Trenches	16	retaliation
19	12.1pm	1.15pm	48th + 71st X	Madally Low farm Mad pt Hindenburg tr	50	u.registration

20	This morning, one gun M.B.		Madagascar tr	3	rd

21	1.35pm till 2.40pm	59th Siege	A 30 c 9.4	19	registration

F. Rodd
Ag. 41? Bd.

GROUP DIARY.

B.

DATE – DEC 4TH 1915

General. Observation was possible 9.40 AM till 3.45 PM. Between the showers the light was good and best of all 1.30 PM 2.30 PM. The enemy were observed using the LA BASSÉE ROAD A22 a 8.7 about midday. And also in neighbourhood of CANTELEUX at 4.30 PM yesterday and 10 to 11.30 AM to-day.

Enemy's Works. Enemy were seen carrying hurdles up CANTELEUX ALLEY SOUTH at 2 PM. A pump has been located working in ENEMY'S front line trench A 16 a 2.5 1.30 PM. All these targets were at once engaged.

Action.

No.	Time. From.	To.	Battery.	Target.	Rounds.	Remarks.
(1)	10 AM	11.30 AM	56	CANTELEUX	6	Enemy seen in the open
(2)	10 AM		71	A 16 a 4 6	15	Retaliation
(3)	11 AM		16	A 21 b 8 8	13	TRENCH MORTAR ACTIVE
(4)	10.35 AM		56	Battery active A 18 a 1 1	20	
(5)	1.37 PM		56	A 16 a 2 5	15	Enemy pumping
(6)	1.45 PM		50	Single truck	8	Retaliation
(7)	2 PM		71	CANTELEUX ALLEY SOUTH	5	Enemy seen
(8)	2.15 PM		71	A 16 a 4.9	15	New work
(9)	2.10 PM		59 SIEGE	A 30 c 9.4	19	Retaliation
(10)	3.15 PM		71	CANTELEUX	27	

B Quiller Couch
Lieut & Adj
for Lieut.Colonel.
Commanding A Group.

1578

DAILY AMMUNITION RETURN

DATE 4th Decr 1915

BATTERIES.

Piece	Projectile	Code	50	70	15	48	71	9	16	17	47	56	Total	Per Piece
18-pr	Guns......													
	Shrapnel...	"A"	29	–	147	225	8	4	38	69	–	–	520	
	H. E.	"Ax"	19	–	–	49	39	7	8	84	–	–	206	
4.5"	Howitzers..													
	Shrapnel...	"B"									–	–	–	
	H. E.	"Bx"									27	31	58	

R.A., 2nd Division Situation - 4-12-1915.

GROUP.	UNIT.	BATTERY POSITION.	WAGON LINE.
-	34th Brigade H.Q.		BETHUNE (Rue St.Pry).
A.	50th Battery	F.18.a.3.2.	F.13.c.9.9.
A.	70th Battery	F.24.c.8.4.	F.13.c.9.9.
A.	36th Brigade H.Q.	A.19.d.3.2.	
Z.	15th Battery	G. 8.a.0.5.	F.14.a.5.2.
Z.	48th Battery	A.25.b.1.8.	F.14.a.5.2.
A.	71st Battery	F.18.a.8.8.(4)	E.5.a.5.10.
Z.		A.14.c.2.6.(2)	
Z.	41st Brigade H.Q.	A.19.d.5.3.	
Z.	9th Battery	F.18.c.3.1.	F. 7.a.7.8.
H.A.	16th Battery	F.24.c.9.2.	W.26.b.3.3.
Z.	17th Battery	F.24.a.8.2.	F.13.d.2.10.
-	44th Brigade H.Q.		BETHUNE.
	47th Battery	F.30.c.7.2.	W.21.c.9.2.
A.	56th Battery	A.20.a.5.8.	CHAMP DE MARS.
Z. A.	7th Mountain Bty.	(A.14.b.2.3.(1) (A.20.a.6.4.(1) (A.26.d.9.2.(2)	F.8.b.
-	59th Siege Battery	F.30.c.5.6.	- -
-	34th D.A.C.		E.18.b.5.5.
-	36th B.A.C.		W.29.b.5.8.
-	41st B.A.C.		E.18.b.9.3.
-	44th B.A.C.		CHAMP DE MARS.
-	D.A.C.		E.21.a.

1st Army No. O/86.
1st Corps No.1/C.A./32.
2nd Divn. No.G.S.86.

G.O.C., R.A., 1st Corps.
─────────────────

      The following method of dealing with a 'Cupola' many of which are being erected by the enemy, is of interest.

      On the morning of the 27th instant, a cupola, situated just behind the German front line opposite the front held by the 11th Corps, was observed for the first time.

      On the 28th instant, 4.5" howitzers of the Guards Division engaged it, and sandbags and parapet round it were completely cleared, so that about 6 feet of wall was visible. Only one round hit the cupola, and this glanced off and did no damage. An 18 pr. battery was then turned on to it, and made what appeared to be a large hole in the side, about three-quarters of the way up.

      From this, it appears that 18 prs. can deal suitably with these cupolas when they are close to the front line, and observation therefore easy. Those at a distance no doubt require treatment with heavier guns.

Adv. First Army.
30th Novr, 1915.

(sd) F. MERCER,
M.G., R.A.

(2).

34th F.A. Brigade.
36th "   "
41st "   "
44th "   "
─────────────────

For information.

R.A., 2nd Divn.
4-12-1915.

Major, R.A.,
Brigade Major, R.A., 2nd Divn.

2nd Divisional Artillery Orders

by

Brigadier-General G.H.SANDERS, D.S.O., Comdg.R.A., 2nd Divn.

4th December, 1915.

1158. STOVES.

The issue of 5 SOYER stoves to each Brigade has been approved. Brigades should draw these direct from D.A.D.O.S.

1159. APPOINTMENTS.

(a). The following are appointed S.S.Corporals with effect from dates stated :-

No.24888, S.S. H.Fenlon, 17th Battery, vice "Alcock" 6-11-1915 and posted to 9th Battery.
No.48300, S.S. Rhone, 9th Battery, vice "Rook" 26-11-15 and posted to 41st B.A.C.
No.67359, S.S. J.Marlow, 9th Battery, vice "Gibbard" 26-11-1915 and posted to 17th Battery.

(b). No.52330 Gr.H.Hole appointed Shoeing-Smith and posted to 17th Battery, vice "Fenlon" 6-11-1915.

1160. DIVINE SERVICE.

The following Divine Services will be held to-morrow 5th December, 1915 :-

(a). CHURCH OF ENGLAND.....9-30 a.m. Unfinished Chapel RUE d'AIRE.
(b). Roman Catholic   .....9-30 a.m. BETHUNE CATHEDRAL.
(c). Wesleyans & Free Church, 9-15 a.m. Div.Recreation Room RUE de Treilles. BETHUNE.
(d) Evening Service (CE.) 6 p.m. RUE D'AIRE.Chapel.
                    (Wes) 6 p.m. Div.Recreation Room RUE d'AIRE.

A. DURAND   Lieutenant R.F.A.

Acting Staff Captain R.A.2nd Divn.

2nd Divisional Artillery
HOSTILE FIRE REPORT.

5th December, 1915.

GENERAL INFORMATION.

59th Siege saw flashes behind ridge near A 30 c 9.4 and fired accordingly.

A base was picked up near No.4 gun, 17th Battery, 8" in diameter with a base fuze marked Kz.Bd.Z 10. Sp 15, R 789
2/V 1/V O/V.

Bombardment by 15th Div.Arty. provoked considerable retaliation from Field Guns about 1 p.m. to 2 p.m.

From marks in the ground Field Guns firing on the LA BASSEE road have a magnetic bearing of 115 deg. from A 19 d 5.4.

HOSTILE FIRE.

No	Time From	To	Nature	Direction from	Area shelled.	Remarks.
1	9-15a	9-30a	77mm	?	VAUXHALL Br	20 rounds.
2	9-20a	9-30a	,,	?	Vicinity RIDGE He	11 ,,
3	10-0 a	10-20a	,,	?	A 15 b 1.2	10 ,,
4	10-45a	11-30a	,, 105mm	AUCHY or behind.	Zo trenches	15th By & 59th Siege retaliated About 200 rds 105 mm fell. It was an organized demonstration by the Germans.
5	11-10a		77mm	AUCHY	CAMBRIN	20 rounds.
6	11-30a	12-15p	,,	S part of LA BASSEE	PONT FIXE	
7	11-30a		,,	AUCHY	X rds VERMELLES	8 rounds
8	12-20p		,,	?	Trs.A 21 c 9.6	6 rounds
9	1-15p	1-45p	,,	AUCHY	A 19 d	30 rounds
10	1-50p	2-0 p	,,) 4.2")	Auchy? A21 d	(LA BASSEE rd from) (20 c 9.8 to 19 d) (6.4)	12 rds 77 mm 2 rds 4.2".
11	2-0 p	3-30p	77mm	AUCHY?	( ) ( ) ( )	Intermittently the whole time several casualties.
12	2-10p		77mm	AUCHY	15th Position.	Retaliate HAISNES
13	2-15p	2-45p	,,	,,	A 20 d	Main road
14	2-15p	3-30p	8"	CANTELEUX	WALKER's Rd.	2 rds @ 5-10 min interval.
15	2-30p	3-15p	77mm	AUCHY	PONT FIXE HARLEY St.	30 rounds.
16	3-0 p		,,	AUCHY	A 2 Trenches	
17	3-0p		5.9"	HAISNES	A 23 d 5.8	
18	3-35p		8"	?	CAMBRIN	3 rounds
19	3-40p		4.2"	?	,,	
20	3-50p		5.9"	?	,, nr Church	3 rounds

German Balloon up at 3-40p true bearing from A 20 c 4.7 is 77 degrees.

Major R.A.
B. M. R. A. 2nd Dn.

GROUP DIARY.

B.

DATE - DEC 5TH 1915.

General. Observation possible 7.AM - 3.45 PM
Light fair after 11 AM.
Enemy seen working on CULVERT
at 9.40 AM.
Enemy were seen working on the Embankment
at 2.25 PM and fired on. And parties
were seen walking from CANTELEUX ALLEY
Enemy's Works. SOUTH to A17C 9.8

'NIL'

Action.

No.	Time From.	To.	Battery.	Target.	Rounds.	Remarks.
(1)	9.15 AM		71	CANTELEUX	20	Retaliation Working Party
(2)	9.40 AM		56	CULVERT	?	
(3)	9.40 AM	11 A	M'T'N B'T'Y	Reserve Trenches behind Brickstacks	20	Retaliation
(4)	10 AM		71	A 17 a 6.6	15	
(5)	11.30 AM		71	M.G. Loophole	15	"
(6)	12 noon		50	FALSE CULVERT	10	
(7)	12.25	12.45	50	ENEMY working in their Front Trench N of CANAL	30	"
(8)	2.20 PM		16	A 22 d.	12	Enemy firing at Aeroplane
(9)	3.15 PM		16	A 21 b 6 3	4	
(10)	3.30 PM		56	A 16 a 2 5	7	
(11)	"		71	ENEMY in open between CANTELEUX ALLEY South & CANAL	25	

B. Quiller Couch
Lieut & Adjt
for Lieut.Colonel.
Commanding A Group.

Strong point destroyed this week. By 48th Divn.

A "cupola" was reported by infantry near pt 79. (A 27 I 7 9) This proved to be only an earthwork no signs of any concrete etc were observed and it does not seem to have any significance although much fresh earth has been thrown up there & new comm trenches leading up to it. 106 rds H.E. were fired and it was considerably damaged also the parapet.

5-12-15

Rodolph
Ag: 41st Bde

B.

GROUP DIARY,

DATE -5-12-15

General.

The same black dog who was reported as dispersed on 2-12-15 reappeared near MINE Point. It will be remembered he was last seen near GIBSONS crater.

CORRECTION:- Considerable activity activity as reported. The 8" shells should have been reported as from direction of CANTELEUX and not from A30 c 9.4 as was done.

Enemy's Works.

- Fresh earth has been thrown up along E side of Railway from about A28 b 20.45 Northwards.

  The cupola reported by infantry near 27 B 79 is dealt with separately by 48th Bat who engaged it today.

- A german was seen near A28 b 20.45 wearing a Khaki coat and dark cap with leather peak.
  Some more posts have been put in along Mad alley A 28 b 9.3.
  Some germans seen digging in a hollow F A 28 b 4.4.

Action.

No.	Time. From.	To.	Battery.	Target.	Rounds.	Remarks.
1	During night		9th Batt	E of ETNA	bursts of fire	
2	7.am			Germans in small parties on Haines La bassee road	12	
3	7.30am	8 am		moving south A24 10 b A 23 b 10.10 small parties of germans moving towards HAINES wearing great coats and packs	35	Several were seen to fall!
4	11.30 am			Trenches	10	retaliation
5	6.30 pm	} 4-12-15	15th Batt	Mad alley	12	by order
6	10.15 pm				12	" "
7	10.30 pm	"		Madagascar	21	by request of infantry
8	11.20 pm	"		"	15	" "

Lieut.Colonel.
Commanding Group.

9.	10.45am till 11.30am	5-12-15	15th Batt	Madagascar	183	in retaliation to demonstration
10.	2 pm			Haines	13	retaliation to fire on Cambrin
11.	2.45 pm			"	24	" "

12	7 pm	4-12-15	47th Batt	Com.tr A29a90.25	6	by orders Z group
13	2 pm			BRANCH Keep	8	registration
14	3.30 pm			HAINES + roads	24	retaliation to german 8" on Auchy quin

15	11 am. 12 noon	48th Batt	Railway tr Hindenburg tr	22	retaliation to shelling Vermelles
16	2 pm - 3 pm		Work see report 1064E		
17	3.30 pm		Railway tr	30	to keep germans from firing at one of our aeroplanes which was flying very low. This appeared to succeed

18	11.15 am	71st Section	Mad alley	12	
19	3 pm		Auchy	20	retaliation to shelling Cambrin

20	7.25 am	17th Batt	Lone farm	9	working party
21	7.40 am		Snipers post	4	
22	10.25 am		Trenches	6	" "
23	11.2 am		Trenches	9	
24	12.10 pm		"	17	" "
25	2.5 pm		"	18	retaliation
26	2.25 pm		"	12	"

27	11.25 am	59th Siege	A28 c 10.7	5	retaliation to demonstration
28	12 noon		A 30 c 9.4	18	registration
29	2.30 pm		HAINES CANTELEUX	5	retaliation to 8"

X Mountain battery moved out.

T. Todd h
Ag. Z group.

DAILY AMMUNITION RETURN

DATE 5.12.15

BATTERIES.

Piece	Projectile	Code	50	70	15	48	71	9	16	17	47	56	Total	Per Piece
18-pr	Guns......													
	Shrapnel...	"A"	15	61	230	167	21	65	24	40	–	–	623	
	H.E.......	"Ax"	3	–	82	21	17	10	5	18	–	–	156	
4.5"	Howitzers..													
	Shrapnel...	"B"									–	–	–	
	H.E.......	"Bx"									11	35	46	

"A" Form.
Army Form C. 2121.
MESSAGES AND SIGNALS. No. of Message..........

Prefix Code m	Words	Charge	This message is on a/c of :	Rec'd at 1555 m
Office of Origin and Service Instructions.	Sent		Service	Date
	At m.			From
	To			By
	By		(Signature of "Franking Officer.")	

TO — Ra 1st Corps

| Sender's Number. | Day of Month. | In reply to Number | AAA |
| * Mo 9+9 | 5 | | |

Ballistite cartridges for 4.5 normally burst short 75 yards at 3000 aaa In colder weather up to 150 yards short aaa 500 yards short has occurred but only recorded by one battery aaa no connection with damp is ~~a feches~~ noticed aaa

From Ra 2 Div
Place
Time 7.35 pm

J Murray Major

The above may be forwarded as now corrected. (Z)
Censor. Signature of Addressor or person authorised to telegraph in his name.

*This line should be erased if not required.

S E C R E T.   2nd Division No: G.S. 778

2nd Division.

No. 1/C.A./34.   5th December, 1915.

(i).   No. 7 Mountain Battery will be withdrawn from the line during night 6th/7th December, preparatory to despatch oversea.

(ii).   It will concentrate at OBLINGHEM, and on 9th December will march with its section of ammunition column via ROBECQ - ST VENANT - MORBECQUE to HAZEBROUCK. An officer to report in advance to the Town Major HAZEBROUCK for billets.

(iii).   On 10th December it will continue its march via WALLON CAPPEL - and BAVINCHOVE to OEHTEZEELE where it will join No.2 and No.5 Mountain Batteries.

(iv).   It will leave 1st Corps area rationed up to 11th December inclusive.

(v).   Supply lorries will join 2nd Army Troops Supply Column at BAVINCHOVE on 10th December after dumping in HAZEBROUCK.

(vi).   No.7 Mountain Battery will report by wire to 1st Corps, feeding strength and numbers and nature of ammunition taken from 1st Army.

(vii).   Acknowledge.

                                            (Sd) R.L.BARTON, Major. R.A.
                                            for Brigadier-General,
                                            General Staff, 1st Corps.

(2).

R.A. 2nd Division.

For information and necessary action.

2nd Division.   Major,
5th December, 1915.   General Staff, 2nd Div.

S E C R E T. 2nd Division No: G.S. 778.

2nd Division.

No. 1/C.A./34.   5th December, 1915.

(i). No.7 Mountain Battery will be withdrawn from the line during night 6th/7th December, preparatory to despatch oversea.

(ii). It will concentrate at OBLINGHEM, and on 9th December will march with its section of ammunition column via ROBECQ - ST VENANT - MORBECQUE to HAZEBROUCK. An officer to report in advance to the Town Major HAZEBROUCK for billets.

(iii). On 19th December, it will continue its march via WALLON CAPPEL - and BAVINCHOVE to OEHTEZEELE where it will join No.2 and No.5 Mountain Batteries.

(iv). It will leave 1st Corps area rationed up to 11th December, inclusive.

(v). Supply lorries will join 2nd Army Troops Supply Column at BAVINCHOVE on 10th December after dumping in HAZEBROUCK.

(vi). No.7 Mountain Battery will report by wire to 1st Corps, feeding strength and numbers and nature of ammunition taken from 1st Army.

(vii). Acknowledge.

(Sd) R.L.BARTON, Major. R.A.
for Brigadier-General,
General Staff, 1st Corps.

(2).
7th Mtn. Battery.
~~Every 2nd Division.~~

For action.

                                       Major R.A.
5th December, 1915.   Brigade Major, R.A., 2nd Div.

2nd Division No. G.S. 744/2.

2nd Division.

No. 1/C.A./23(2). 5th Dec.1915.

1. The training of the East Anglian Artillery will recommence on Tuesday 7th instant.

2. On that date the personnel of two 18 pdr. sections and one howitzer section will be attached to the artillery of each of the divisions in the front line.

3. Details to be arranged direct between East Anglian Artillery and the Divisions concerned.

(Sgd) J.K.DICK-CUNYINGHAM. Major.
for Brigadier-General.
General Staff, 1st Corps.

2.

R.A., 2nd Division.

For information and necessary action.

2nd Division.
6th December, 1915.

Major.
General Staff, 2nd Div.

"A" Form. Army Form C.2121.

MESSAGES AND SIGNALS.

Prefix	Code	m	Words	Charge	This message is on a/c of:	Recd. at 15 58 m.
Office of Origin and Service Instructions.			Sent		Service.	Date
			At m.			From
			To			By
			By		(Signature of "Franking Officer.")	

TO — A Group 59th Siege

Sender's Number.	Day of Month.	In reply to Number	AAA
Bm 995	5		

It is believed that the Germans will
relieve their troops in front line at 6 am
tomorrow 6th inst

A group will enfilade PLUM ALLEY TOWPATH
ALLEY and CANAL BANK with 18 pr shrapnel
if called on. N7 central and also Trench
shed SE of CANTELEUX Shown on Sketch
map issued with 1st Corps summary of News.
About 200 rounds on stokes area 4.5
Howitzers and 6 in howitzer with Inward
Earthwork A9 a on N5 200 rounds also Bm.
50 rounds each. Fire will be in burst
from 5.15 am till daylight ...

B be firing on or pointing with
gun are to from as reported by the
R.F.C.

From Ra e Dir
Place
Time 19 Mrs

The above may be forwarded as now corrected. (Z)

Censor. Signature of Addressor or person authorised to telegraph in his name.
* This line should be erased if not required.

"A" Form. — MESSAGES AND SIGNALS. — Army Form C. 2121.

TO: 2nd Div G

Sender's Number: BM 940
Day of Month: 5
AAA

In order to catch enemy's relief at 6 am tomorrow 6th following programme has been arranged —

18 pdrs Enfilade PLAIN ALLEY TOWPATH ALLEY and CANAL BANK and tracks S & SE of LANTELY
200 rounds

4.5 howitzers fire on work A 17 a — 100 rounds

6 in howitzers fire — — — 50 rounds

12th Division Artillery cooperate to north. 60 pdr cooperate on approaches further E. Fire from 5.15 am till daylight in bursts ...

From: RA 2 Div
Place:
Time: 10.15 am

2nd Divisional Artillery Orders

by

Brigadier-General G.H.SANDERS, D.S.O., Comdg.R.A., 2nd Divn.

5th December, 1915.

1161. WINDSCREENS.

A return showing in detail the requirements of each unit in windscreens will be rendered to this office as soon as possible.

A.DURAND, Lieut.R.A.,
a/Staff Captain, R.A., 2nd Divn.

GROUP DIARY.

DATE - DEC 6TH 1915.

General. The "Sharps" this morning evidently interested considerably with M. Lunny's shells N of the Canal. At 7.15 AM when distant observation became possible considerable parties of the enemy being packs were seen at CANTALEUX and ROCH ALLEY meeting point. They were engaged by the 4.5 How: & 70th Batty who put some shots into them causing

Enemy's Works.
several casualties. The enemy did not succeed getting out of his

9.15 A.17.a — It provoked considerable retaliation on our trench between DUCKS BILL & CANAL from 8.30 AM to 10.30 AM

The light was exceptionally good from 7.30 AM till 2.30 PM.

Action.

No.	Time From.	To.	Battery.	Target.	Rounds.	Remarks.
(1)	4.15 A	7.15 A	A 50 71 / 56 69 S	TOW PATH CANTELEUX ALLEY CANAL BANK Tracks A.17.a	As per programme
(2)	7.15 A	3.20 P	56	Enemy in open A.11.a & b A.10.d	81	Almost always some movement
(3)	7.30	8 A	50	" "	12	
(4)	9 A		71	ENEMY in open near A.17.a 67	20	
(5)	10 A		50	A.17.a 67	6	
(6)	1.50 P		56	Pump working A.16.a 2.5	8	
(7)	3 PM		50	Periscopes visible in TORTOISE & EMBANKMENT	6	
(8)	11 AM	12 noon	M'T'N B'T'Y	Brick stacks	28	

B. Quiller Couch
Lieut & Adj
for Lieut. Colonel.
Commanding A Group.

Z GROUP DIARY.

B.

DATE - 6-12-15

General.

There seems to have been a relief this morning as many parties of germans were seen walking about between Aucky and the CORONS with greatcoats and packs. They appear to use the roads in the early morning. Long was the list of slain. Several batteries got on to them.

Enemy's Works.

Fresh earth has been thrown up between A.29.b.90.85.75 and A.29.b.15.20

Fresh concertina wire has been placed between A.21.d.6.4 and A.21.a.70.55.

Action.

No.	Time From.	To.	Battery.	Target.	Rounds.	Remarks.
1	7.30 am	8.15 am	9th	Road A.18.c.1.1	20	parties of germans.
2	9.15 am			A.18.d parties of germans proceeding towards La Bassee having apparently come out of the trenches	35	very effective numerous corpses.
3	12 noon			A.19.a.0.5	few	movement
4	3.15 pm			Franks heap	10	retaliation
5	10.20 am		15th Bat	Auw trenches	14	Retaliation
6	11.20 am			" "	14	"
7	1.30 pm			" "	11	"
8	2 pm				34	
9	2 pm			mad alley	12	Registration
10	2.15 pm			" "	3	"
11	2.30 pm			" "	12	"

Lieut.Colonel.
Commanding Group.

12	7.20 am	17th Batt	Working party	5 rds.?		
13	8.20 am		trenches	5		These parties
14	8.40 am		" "	5		were probably
15	9.25 am		" "	7		relieving in
16	9.45 am		" "	14		trenches.
17	9.55 am		" "	7		
18	10.47 am		" "	7		
			" "	6	retaliation	
19	12.25 pm		Snipers post	11		
20	1.58 pm		" "	13		
21	2.7 pm		A30a 1.5	20	working party	
22	2.30 pm		Front tr.	13	german building up parapet	
~~23~~	~~2.45 pm~~					

23	7.22 am 7.49 am	47th Batt	A29a 85.25	10	working party dispersed
24	11.38 am 12.17 pm		A29a 85.25	14	" "
25	2.47 pm		Mad alley A28 69.3	10	retaliation
26	3.16 pm		Ryans keep	3	

27	8.30 am	48th Batt	Mine point	6	
28	10.25 am		Railway tr	14	retaliation
29	11 am		Mine point	3	retaliation
30	1.30 pm		Mine point	16	working party
31	1.45 pm		Railway tr	20	retaliation
32	3 pm		Mine pt.	12	"
33	3.30 pm		" and Auchy	14	"
34	4 pm		"	8	

35	3 pm	59th Siege	A28 6 8 6	2	registration

Rodd...
Adj. 41½ Bn.

2nd Divisional Artillery

HOSTILE FIRE REPORT.

6th December, 1915.

NO.	Time From	To	Nature	Direction From	Aera Shelled	Remarks.
1	8-30a	10-30a	77mm	CANTELEUX	Front Line and GUNNER SIDING.	100 rounds
2	9-0 a	11-45a	5.9"	VIOLAINES	S of WESTMINSTER Bridge road. A 7 d	40 rounds at irregular intervals
3	10-20a		77mm	AUCHY	A 27 b	8 rounds
4	11-15a		77mm	,,	A 21 b	4 rounds
5	1-30p	1-50p	5.9"	,,	VERMELLES rd.	
6	2-0p	2-30p	5.9"	VIOLAINES	As in No.2 above.	25 rounds
7	2-45p	3-30p	77mm	AUCHY	LA BASSEE Rd & Trenches near	A few rounds at intervals.
8	3-0 p		5.9"	VIOLAINES	As in 2 above.	4 rounds.
9	3-15p		77mm	Railway Triangle.	ROBERTSON'S Avenue	10 rounds
10	3-30p		77mm	AUCHY	A 21 d	8 rounds.

Major R.A.

Brigade Major R.A. 2nd Div.

DAILY AMMUNITION RETURN

DATE 6th Decr 1915.

BATTERIES.

Piece	Projectile	Code	50	70	15	48	71	9	16	17	47	56	Total	Per Piece
18-pr	Guns.......													
	Shrapnel...	"A"	212	126	64	133	103	41	14	59	-	-	482	
	H.E.......	"Ax"	44	57	-	132	130	66	-	49	-	-	478	
4.5"	Howitzers..													
	Shrapnel...	"B"									-	-	-	
	H.E.......	"Bx"									47	202	249	

RA 2nd Div.
Maximum Arc of Fire

Reference 1/10000 map

Battery	Position	Bearing True°	
71 4 guns	F 18 a 8.7	73 - 115	42
2 guns	A 14 c 2.6	117 - 141	24
50	F 18 a 5.1	69 - 110	51
16	F 24 c 8.3	51 - 105	54
9	F 24 a 9.4	79 - 111	32
17	F 24 a 6.0	72 - 114	42
48	A 19 d 1.1	73 - 120	47
15	G 7 b 9.4	31 - 74	43
55	A 20 a 5.2	38 - 120	82
47	A 30 c 6.2	50 - 111	61
59 Siege	A 30 c 5.6	24 - 104	80

Ra 2 Div
7.12.15

Newbury Major
BMRA

18	42°
4.5	72°
6"	80°

2nd Divisional Artillery Orders

by

Brigadier-General G.H.SANDERS, D.S.O., Comdg.R.A., 2nd Divn.

6th December,1915.

1162. SANITATION.

All O.C's Units are responsible that the drains by the side of the roads near their billets and wagon lines are kept properly clean.

1163. LAMPS.

The reflector lamps which were issued some ten days ago, at the rate of one per battery, B.A.C. and section D.A.C., were intended to light up the billets of the men, and should not be used for other purposes.

1164. LABELS AND INSULATORS.

R.A.Units in need of labels or insulators can obtain same from O.C., Signals, 2nd Division.

1165. PROMOTION OF S.S.CORPORALS.

A number of Farrier Sergeants are required in Artillery units of the new armies.
The names of qualified S.S.Corporals that can be spared and recommended for posting with a view to filling the vacancies should be sent to this office by 8-0 p.m.,9th December,1915.

L.G.BUXTON, Capt, R.A.,
Staff Captain, R.A., 2nd Divn.

- NOTICE. -

LOST - Dark Bay Mare - height, 14.2 hands - Description :-Batter No113-Star.Blaize - 50 near hind quarters - 50 off fore foot.
Also Black Gelding - height 16 hands - scar near forearm - 50 near hind quarters - 50 off fore foot,- Battery No.21.
Information in both cases to be sent to O.C., 50th Battery R.F.A.

2 Div. RA DIARY.

DATE 7.XII.15

OBSERVATION CONDITIONS. Observation possible 7 am. to 3.50 pm. Light good. Wind S 7 mph. gusty.

WORK DONE BY ENEMY. Haystack at A 28 b 2.6 has been altered.
Some digging has been done behind Vesuvius.
Fresh earth has been thrown up at A 30 a 7.0.
Communication trench A 22 c & d between railway and Auchy improved.

MOVEMENT SEEN. A few Germans were seen this morning on Haines La Bassée road, but not so many as yesterday.
North of Canal enemy exposed themselves frequently - between VIOLAINES and CANTELEUX a party of 30 at 11.45 am wearing full kit moving W. and at gap in hedge A 10 b 7.0 a party of 50 moving W. at 1 pm in single file in full kit.

GUNS LOCATED OR SUSPECTED.
    4 5.9" howitzers at about A 18 a 3.3 or 1.1
    77 battery at about A 18 a 8.4

WORK DONE BY US. Working parties seen -
    One man filling sandbags A 30 b 2.0
    Party digging behind crater A 21 d 6.4
    A trench has been dug through the ruins of Lean to Cottage.

GENERAL. The tree at PLUME TREE Ho. has been cut down by a shell from 59th Siege.
    A Battery of 77 mm guns in N. Auchy very active all day. Could not be located. Direction by sound only.
    O.P. was noticed yesterday at A 23 a 1.3 in a house - 60 rounds H.E. were fired on it and house is now considerably damaged.

There is a mound on canal bank at A 15 d 8.7 with what is thought to be a cupola and a slit faced NW.

ACTION.   See Over.

                                Lt. Colonel Major
                                Commanding

ACTION Time From	To	Battery	Target	Rounds	Remarks
9.25		15	New trenches	8	Retaliation
2.30	3.45		Madagascar & Support trenches	207	Retaliation for heavy shelling
3.15	4		Haisnes	14	" " Shelling Vermelles
10p		48	Dock & Mad alley	12	
12.15a			Douvrin	5	
11.10a	12.15p		Auchy	25	Destruction of house
2.30p	2.45p		Dock & Chateau Alley	6	Retaliation
3p			Railway dock & tc.	40	Destruction and retaliation
3.20p			Dock Alley	2	Retaliation
7.50a		17	Front trench Z2	1	movement
10.5			"	4	"
3.45			"	8	"
7.30a		9	A29 b 3 6	20	work party dispersed
1.30p			A 23 a 1.3	60	OB demolished
10a		50	False Culvert	6	
3.35p	3.45p		Embankment redoubt, trucks & Triangle	40	retaliation
7p	7.30p	71	CANTELEUX & LA BASSEE	20	
8.30a			A 17a 5.6	15	
10.15a			TORTOISE	15	Retaliation
1.15p			CANTELEUX	15	"
2.45p			A 15 d 8.7	5	Mound
7.30p		47 How	A29 a 9½ 2½	2	To catch regular work here
8.20a			A29 a 9½ 3	16	working party
10a	12 noon		Branch Keep	40	Aeroplane registration
2.35p			Auchy	11	Register an earthwork
2.51p			A28 b 3.5 trench	9	registration
10.15a		56 How	False Culvert	6	
2.30p			A 18 a 1.1	14	Battery
9.10a	11.30a	59 Siege	Plume Tree Ho.	35	Further destruction
2.30p			Ho. A23a 1.3	6	registration
3p			A 28 C	15	retaliation
1.30p		71 detached Section	work on railway in front of Les Briques	30	weekly destruction of strong point

2nd Divisional Artillery
HOSTILE FIRE REPORT.

7th December, 1915.

1. **GENERAL INFORMATION.**

   One particular battery in N.Auchy 77 mm. was very active all day, but no flash could be observed. Direction judged by sound only.

2. **HOSTILE FIRE.**

No.	Time. From	Time. To	Nature.	Direction from	Area shelled.	Remarks.
1.	9-15 a		77 m.m.	AUCHY.	Railway A.27.d.	10 Rounds.
2.	10-15 a		,,	,,	Vermelles - La Bassee Rd. A.27.a.	2 Rounds.
3.	10-15 a		10.5 c.m.	?	HOLLOW	8 Rounds.
4.	10-15 a		10.5 c.m.	VIOLAINES	SPOIL BANK.	6 Rounds.
5.	10-30 a		10.5 c.m.	S.of LA BASSEE.	ANNEQUIN.	20 Rounds.
6.	11-30 a	11-55 a	105 m.m.	-	VERMELLES.	12 Rounds.
7.	1-5 p		77 m.m.	CANTELEUX	A.8.d.8.3.	
8.	1-20 p	1-30 p	105 m.m.	-	VERMELLES.	6 Rounds.
9.	1-23 p	2-30 p	77 m.m.	N.AUCHY.	TOURBIERES LOOP.	6 Rounds.
10.	1-45 p	2-15 p	10.5 c.m.	?	TOURBIERES & ANNEQUIN.	30 Rounds.
11.	2-0 p	3-15 p	77 m.m.	N.AUCHY SIMS Keep & Opp. Railway tr.	Railway ?	150 Rounds.
12.	2-30 p	3-0 p	105 m.m. H.E.	Distillery DOUVRIN(?)	TOURBIERES LOOP.	1 Round a minute.
13.	2-30 p		77 m.m.	A.18,a.1.1.	N.CUINCHY & PONT FIXE,	
14.	2-50 p	3-15 p	105 m.m. Shrap.	?	LA BASSEE - VERMELLES Road.	20 Rounds.
15.	3-15 p	3-30 p	77 m.m.	AUCHY.	Opp. Rly tr.	
16.	3-30 p		77 m.m.	?	CUINCHY & PONT FIXE.	

Query p.m.?

Major, R.A.,
Brigade Major,

1567

DAILY AMMUNITION RETURN

DATE 7.12.15

BATTERIES.

Piece	Projectile	Code	50	70	15	48	71	9	16	17	47	56	Total Per Piece
18-pr	Guns......												
	Shrapnel...	"A"	7	66	53	112	22	76	-	58	-	-	394
	H. E.......	"Ax"	18	33	-	32	70	28	-	63	-	-	244
4.5"	Howitzers..												
	Shrapnel...	"B"									3		3
	H. E.......	"Bx"									72	56	128

"A" Form.
MESSAGES AND SIGNALS.
Army Form C. 2121.

Prefix...... Code......m.	Words	Charge	This message is on a/c of:	Recd. at......m.
Office of Origin and Service Instructions.	Sent			Date......
	At......m.		......Service.	From......
	To......			By......
	By......		(Signature of "Franking Officer.")	

TO: 15th Division / 1st Corps

Sender's Number: ...... Day of Month: ...... In reply to Number: ...... AAA

1st Corps has placed heavy artillery at disposal of 2nd Div for bombardment opposite A section on 9th Dec aaa Details of bombardment have been communicated to all concerned aaa 5th Infy Bde and 1st Mining Co RE will start clearing front line system at 9am and will notify OC A artillery group when all is clear aaa limits of area to be evacuated will be settled direct between OC 5th Bde and OC A artillery group aaa Bombardment will commence when infantry are clear about 10 am and will continue until about 3pm aaa OC A artillery group is responsible for informing 5 Inf Bde and 1st Co RE when bombardment is over and line can be reoccupied aaa Addressees RA 5th Bde and 1st Mining Co RE repeated 6th Bde 1st Corps 5th Div and 2nd Div

From: 2 Div
Place:
Time:

The above may be forwarded as now corrected. (Z)

Censor. Signature of Addressor or person authorised to telegraph in his name.
* This line should be erased if not required.

"A" Form.
MESSAGES AND SIGNALS.

Army Form C. 2121.

Prefix	Code	m.	Words	Charge	This message is on a/c of:	Recd. at ...... m.
Office of Origin and Service Instructions.			Sent			Date
Secret			At ...... m.		...... Service.	From
Depot			To			
			By		(Signature of "Franking Officer.")	By

TO RA 2nd Div

Sender's Number	Day of Month	In reply to Number	
* G826	8		A A A

Proposals for operations on BRICKSTACKS tomorrow are approved by Corps Commander aaa 33rd Siege Battery and 1 Section 10th Siege Battery are placed at disposal of 2nd Division aaa This artillery will be under orders GOC RA 2nd Division

From 2nd Div
Place
Time 7.35 pm

R. Belgrave

2nd Divisional Artillery Orders

by

Brigadier-General G.H.SANDERS, D.S.O., Comdg.R.A., 2nd Divn.

7th December, 1915.

1166. FIELD OVENS.

Field ovens can be drawn from C.R.E. at the rate of one per unit. These ovens will be built up at the billets and will remain as a permanent store of that billet.

1167. FRENCH WAR LOAN.

Any officer, N.C.O., or man who wishes to subscribe to the "Emprunt de défense nationale" (French War Loan) can obtain full particulars from this office.

1168. LEAVE.

The now allotment of leave is as follows:-

Thursday	30 men	D.A.C.
Friday	18 "	36th Brigade.
	7 "	44th "
	3 "	34th "
	1 "	Armoured Cars.
	1 "	Spare.
Saturday.	18 "	41st Brigade.
	6 "	34th "
	6 "	D.A.C.
Sunday.	30 "	34th Brigade.
Monday.	30 "	36th "
Tuesday.	30 "	41st "
Wednesday.	30 "	44th "

L.G.BUXTON, Capt, R.A.,

Staff Captain, R.A., 2nd Divn.

2 Div RA DIARY.

DATE 8.XII.15

OBSERVATION CONDITIONS. Observation possible 7.10 am — 4 pm. Light good. Wind W to WSW 10 mh.

WORK DONE BY ENEMY.

MOVEMENT SEEN. Small parties seen walking in open Auchy — Dump 7 am. Movement to and fro in open near CANTELEUX 10 — 12.5 pm. Twos and threes moving across open CANTELEUX — LA BASSÉE 1 pm — 1.20 pm.
6 men going towards CANTELEUX from A10a91 9.6 — 9.30 am

GUNS LOCATED OR SUSPECTED.
Battery supposed at A17d 4½.3 active 10.45 am

WORK DONE BY US.

GENERAL. Flag seen flying from house B14a0.5. Two Germans one in long grey cloak the other in dark clothes were seen to enter. The house was shelled. Flag about 2 ft long of a dingy colour.
House in A23a1.3 further treated today. The roof is of sheet iron with 2' of brick over. The wall 3' from sand bag work inside. Further treatment required.
House A17c2.3 has look out holes in face. Two good hits with H.E. made.
A hostile aeroplane flew over very low and passed immediately overhead at the moment that a mine was exploded near DUCKS BILL.
There was a certain amount of hostile activity for which we retaliated on various points.

ACTION. See Over.

Murray Major
Lt. Colonel.
Commanding
2nd D RA

ACTION

Time From	To	Battery	Target	Rounds	Remarks
9.30		15	HAISNES	16	Retaliation
10.45		"	"	12	"
7p			"	20	"
11.30			Snipers Post A28c01	38	"
3.30p			Madagascar Tr.	16	"
4.15p			Brickstacks	16	Registration
7a		48	Lean To Cottage Chateau alley Mad alley	22	To catch movement
10.20	10.30		Trench Z1	40	Retaliation
12.30p			Madagascar Tr.	26	"
2.30p			Auchy alley	42	Registration
			Pekin alley		
3.50p			Madagascar Tr.	10	Retaliation
7.30a		17	Pekin tr.	5	Movement
7.35a			Front trench Z2	12	Working party
8.10a			Haisnes Road	1	Movement
9			Front Z2	3	
9.15a			"	5	work
10.30			Pekin tr.	3	
10.50			Haisnes	50	Retaliation
3.25p			Snipers Post	10	
3.45p			Front Z2	5	instruction
7.50a		9	A29b 3.6	12	working party dispersed
10.50a			Triangle	5	Retaliation
1.36p			A23a 1.3 OP	50	Treatment continued
1.45p			B19a 1½ 5	20	Important Germans
7p		71 detached	Madagascar tr. Railway tr.	25	Retaliation
8.15a		71	Distillery A17d	13	
9.6	9.20		CANTELEUX	20	Movement
11.43	11.50		A17a 6.6 A17a 2.6	50	Retaliation
8.30a	9.30a	50	X road A22 b 9.10	20	Retaliation
10.45			A17d 4.3		
1.	1.20		Enemy in open CANTELEUX	*	
7p			A17d 4.3		
10.20		16	A17d 9.9	10	
3.30	3.45		A17c 2.3		O.P. Suspected
11 a	*	47	A28 6 7.3	7	Aeroplane registration
12.30p			Les Briques A22a 3.2	9	M.G. Emplacement
1.35p			Auchy	26	O.P. - 4 hits
3.10			Branch Keep	1	
8.45	9.20	56	Embankment & Chlost	7	Retaliation
10	12.5		CANTELEUX	10	Movement
10 a		5q Siege	A22 b 8.5	16	Demolition
2.30p			A22 d 9½ 3	29	"

2nd Divisional Artillery

HOSTILE FIRE REPORT.

8th December, 1915.

1. GENERAL INFORMATION.

Batteries supposed to be located A.17.d.4½.3. was observed active about 10-45 a.m. and engaged by 50th Battery.
16th Battery engaged House A.17.c.2.3. where loop-holes were observed, 2 direct hits with very good H.E. detonators.

2. HOSTILE FIRE.

No.	Time From	To	Nature	Direction From	Area shelled	Remarks.
1.	8-55 a	9-20 a	5.9"	?	CUINCHY KINGSCLERE	20 Rds.
2.	9-5 a		77 mm.	?	A,27.a.	15 Rds.
3.	9-6 a	9-30 a	77 mm.	CANTELEUX	A,15.b.1.2.	
4.	10-5 a		4.2" &77 mm.	?	Tr.A.21.d. A.27.b.	15 Rds. 8 Rds.
5.	10-15 a		77 mm.		HARLEY ST.	8 Rds.
6.	11-10 a	11-15 a	77 mm.	CANTELEUX	GIVENCHY	40 Rds.
7.	,,	,,	5.9"	VIOLAINES	,,	6 Rds.
8.	12noon	12-20 p	77 mm. 105 mm.	?	CME trenches A.2 Subsection	
9.	12noon		105 mm.	HAISNES	VERMELLES X	5 Rds.
10.	1-0 p		77 mm.	?	~~A.2 Subsection~~ A.15,b.1.2.	10 Rds.
11.	1-30 p		77 mm.	?	CAMBRIN	
12.	1-45 p	2-15 p	77 mm.	AUCHY	,,	20 Rds.
13.	2-20 p		77 mm.	DISTILLERY A 17 d	HARLEY ST.	
14.	3-45 p		105 mm.	HAISNES	tr.S.VERMELLES Road.	12 Rds.

Major, R.A.,
Brigade Major, R.A., 2nd Divn.

1571

DAILY AMMUNITION RETURN

DATE 8th Decr 1915

BATTERIES.

Piece	Projectile	Code	50	70	15	48	71	9	16	17	47	56	Total Per Piece
18-pr	Guns.......												
	Shrapnel...	"A"	120	37	216	170	10	37	10	76	-	-	676
	H. E.......	"Ax"	-	52	29	27	84	123	-	17	-	-	332
4.5"	Howitzers..												
	Shrapnel...	"B"									-	-	-
	H. E.......	"Bx"									31	164	195

COPY NO. 12.

2nd Division Artillery Operation Order No. 9.

8th December, 1915.

Reference Sheet 36c N.W.1 $\frac{1}{10000}$

1. Weather permitting, a bombardment of certain positions of the enemy's line will be carried out to-morrow, according to the attached programme, beginning at about 10-0 a.m.

2. 1st Corps have placed a portion of the Heavy Artillery, 1st Corps at the disposal of 2nd Division for these operations. The operations will be carried out under the direction of O.C., A.Group. ~~47th Howitzer and~~ 59th Siege are also placed at his disposal.

3. O.C., A.Group will consult with G.O.C., 5th Infantry Brigade as to the weather conditions and will arrange with him for the withdrawal of all infantry and engineers from the trenches as the G.O.C., considers necessary. The bombardment will open as soon as the trenches are cleared.

O.C., A.Group will also inform G.O.C., 5th Infantry Brigade when the bombardment is completed.

Major, R.A.,
Brigade Major, R.A., 2nd Div

Issued at 7.45 to :-
Copy No. 1 A.Group.
  "   2 Z.Group.
  "   3 34th Brigade.
  "   4 44th   "
  "   5 59th Siege Battery.
  "   6 D.A.C.
  "   7&8 2nd Divn. G.
  "   9 H.A., 1st Corps.
  "   10 R.A., 13th Division.
  "   11 R.A., 15th Division.

Unit.	Time.	Target.	Ammunition.	Remarks.
Section 10th) Siege Battery) 33rd Siege Battery)	10-0 a.m. 3-0 p.m. 3-0 p.m. to 4-0 p.m.	Brickstacks A.21.b.8.8. to A.15.d.9.3. Line A.22.a.4.7. to A.16.c.5.3.	) 150))) 400))	To demolish all works specially mine shafts.
59th Siege Battery	10-0 a.m. to 4-0 p.m.	Strong points in support line behind Brickstacks	360.	To demolish all works specially minenwerfer positions Not to fire West of line through A.16.c.4.0. after 3-0 p.m.
50th Field Bty. 18th Field Bty.	10-0 a.m. to 4-30 pm.	Approaches.	600	

2nd Divisional Artillery Orders

by

Brigadier-General G.H.SANDERS, D.S.O.,Comdg.R.A.,2nd Division.

8th December,1915.

1169. COURTMARTIAL.

A F.G.C.M. will assemble at Headquarters, R.A.,2nd Division (18 RUE SADI-CARNOT,BETHUNE) at 10-0 a.m. on Friday, 10th December,1915, for the trial of No.48581. Dr.A.Gibbs,2nd Divisional Ammunition Column, and No.48196.Gr.J.T.Frost,44th Brigade Ammunition Column, and such other accused as may be brought before it :-

PRESIDENT.
Major W.A.F.Jones, 70th Battery, R.F.A.

MEMBERS.
Captain A.L.P.Griffith, D.S.O., 48th Battery, R.F.A.
Lieutenant C.H.Putnam, 9th Battery, R.F.A.

The accused to be warned and all witnesses duly required to attend.
Proceedings to be forwarded to Staff Captain, R.A., 2nd Division.
Court Orderly to be supplied by 2nd Divl.Ammunition Column.

1170. HORSE STANDINGS.

In future any demand for bricks on C.R.E. must state the number of horses for which Standings are required to be made.

1171. HEADCOVER.

Poles for headcover, and brushwood for windscreens are available at 47th Battery Wagon Line W.21.c.9.1. Also tin for roofing at the Armourer's Shop, which is in the street behind 2nd Divn. Q. Office.
Experimental Headcover has been erected at 41st B.A.C. E.18.b.9,4. The Sergeant Major of that Unit will explain to all units which is the best. The best method is the Headcover furthest from the main road.
Poles, brushwood and tins can only be drawn on an order issued from this office. Two wagon loads per unit only will be issued to commence Headcover, and the following units should send a N.C.O. to this Office as soon as possible to receive an order:- 34th B.A.C. 15th,48th, 71st,36th B.A.C.,16th,17th,41st B.A.C.,44th,B.A.C(each section).
Os.C.Brigades are requested to inform this office as soon as possible how many horses can be covered with the above amount of material.

L.G.BUXTON, Capt, R.A.,
Staff Captain, R.A., 2nd Divn.

"A" Form.
Army Form C. 2121.
MESSAGES AND SIGNALS.
No. of Message

| Prefix | Code | m. | Words | Charge | This message is on a/c of: | Recd. at | m. |
| Office of Origin and Service Instructions. | | | Sent At m. To By | | Service. (Signature of "Franking Officer.") | Date 10 From By | |

Priority

| TO | RA 1st Corps | | | |

| Sender's Number. | Day of Month | In reply to Number | AAA |
| 4833 | 9 | | |

Owing to mist bombardment will not take place today aaa date of bombardment will be notified later aaa 5th Bde to inform 2/1st mining co aaa acknowledge aaa addressed RA 5th Inf Bde repeated 1st Corps

From: Inel DW
Place:
Time: 9 15 am

The above may be forwarded as now corrected. (Z)

Censor. Signature of Addressor or person authorised to telegraph in his name.
* This line should be erased if not required.

(T1809) Wt. 14142—641. 45000 pads. 4/15. Sir J. C. & S.

2nd Div. RA DIARY.

DATE 9·XII·15

OBSERVATION CONDITIONS. Observation impossible. Front line occasionally visible. Wind S by E, slight.

WORK DONE BY ENEMY.

MOVEMENT SEEN. One or two enemy seen 9 am at A16a28

GUNS LOCATED OR SUSPECTED.

WORK DONE BY US.

GENERAL. Enemy made a prearranged retaliation to the 15th Division bombardment. Most of it fell on Z₀ Sector. It began one minute after the 15th Div. opened. We retaliated. Otherwise all quiet.

ACTION. See Over.

Murray Major
L⁺ Colonel.
Commanding

ACTION					
Time From	To	Battery	Target	Rounds	Remarks.
		15 17 48 49 59 71	} Trenches		Retaliation
			nothing else of importance()		

ACTION					
Time From	To	Battery	Target	Rounds	Remarks.

2nd Divisional Artillery
HOSTILE FIRE REPORT.

9th December, 1915.

B. HOSTILE FIRE.

No.	Time From	To	Nature	Direction from	Area shelled	Remarks.
1.	8th. 5-0 p		77 mm.	?	GIVENCHY GUNNER Siding	25 Rounds.
2.	8-50 p		77 mm.	?	CUINCHY	20 Rounds.
3.	9th. 11-55 a		77 mm.	LA BASSEE South	GIVENCHY	50 Rounds.
4.	12-15 p	12-40 p	77 mm. 105 mm.	? LA BASSEE	A.26.b.& Vicinity MAISON ROUGE	2 Rounds 4.2" were effective
5.	12-35 p	12-45 p	77 mm. 105 mm.	?	Zo trenches	Retaliation to 15th Division fire.
6.	1-10 p	1-15 p	77 mm.	AUCHY	Barrier on Road	3 Rounds.
7.	1-15 p	1-35 p	77 mm.	?	BRADDELL Pt.	1 Round followed by 2, 1 minute interval.
8.	1-20 p		77 mm.	AUCHY	A. 25 b 5 9	4 Rounds.
9.	3-0 p	3-10 p	77 mm. 105 mm.	?	Zo trenches	Not so heavy as No.5.

L G Burton
for
Brigade Major, R.A.,

Major, R.A.,
2nd Division.

DAILY AMMUNITION RETURN

DATE

BATTERIES.

Piece	Projectile	Code	50	70	15	48	71	9	16	17	47	56	Total Per Piece
18-pr	Guns......												
	Shrapnel...	"A"	44	–	78	126	32	40	21	20			361
	H. E......	"Ax"	5	54	45	47	29	81	–	–			261
4.5"	Howitzers..												
	Shrapnel...	"B"									–	–	–
	H. E......	"Bx"									1	26	27

"A" Form. Army Form C. 2121.
MESSAGES AND SIGNALS.

Prefix	Code	m.	Words	Charge	This message is on a/c of:	Recd. at	m.
Office of Origin and Service Instructions.			Sent			Date	
~~Sent~~			At	m.	Service.	From	
			To			By	
			By		(Signature of "Franking Officer.")		

TO { 59th Siege   A Group
      2 Group

| Sender's Number | Day of Month | In reply to Number | AAA |
| Div 953 | 4 | | |

Plate day on following night

	One gun	A 16 c 3 5
	One gun	A 22 a 6 8
	One gun	A 22 d 1½ 0

addressed 59th Siege repeated
A + 2 Groups aaa

From R.A. 2Div
Place
Time 10.35 am

2nd Divisional Artillery Orders

by

Brigadier-General G.H.SANDERS, D.S.O., Comdg.R.A., 2nd Divn.

9th December, 1915.

1172. STORES.

The Batteries who formerly applied to the 11th Compy. R.E., for stores should now apply to the 226th Field Coy., which has replaced the 11th Coy. and is in the same billet.

1173. ABSENTEES.

The report called for in 2nd Divn.Q.No.4028, R.A.1066, should reach this office by 8-0 p.m. Friday, 10th December, 1915.

L.G.BUXTON, Capt, R.A.
Staff Captain, R.A., 2nd Divn.

2nd Div. R.A Diary
10 Dec 1915

Observation Conditions Observation possible 7 am to 3.45 pm,
light good after 9.30 am. Wind W 20 mph.

Work done by Enemy

Movement Seen (~~Movements~~)
Some ~~time~~ large parties + heavily equipped moving in open, in relief 3.45 pm.
Single men SE of Canteleux throughout the day. They run fast across an open space.
Movement in relief consisted of two parties of 40 passing each other at LES BRIQUES and larger parties by LONE FARM.

Guns located or Suspected
A new battery in ruined houses A 6 d 3.2 firing towards FESTUBERT
Battery (thought H 1 a 7.2) firing from 1.15 – 1.30. Seen from 400 immediately over 3 CABARETS.

Working parties Seen
Party hammering and working NW Corner of NE brickstack. 3 pm
Pumping and digging party A 16 a 2.9 3.5 pm
Party throwing out earth in Embankment redoubt 3.5 pm.
A 17 C 2.2 4.45 pm.

General
It was reported that a relief was in progress in Z front 3.45 pm. Two batteries fired some rapid bursts, searching and sweeping well. No results could be seen (too dark). ~~But~~
Enemy's artillery fairly quiet.
The morning was one favourable for catching enemy moving – intervals of mist and clear.
From movement in open enemy's Communication trenches are judged bad.
Fragment of message from DOUVRIN again read.
White flags seen at A 30 a 7.2 and A 30 a 4.2, thought traces of new trench. Registered.
Road leading north in A 22 d 8.5 seems to be used.

CEHT JEGAND
VON SUCH —
— POST HOLEN C —

Principle Action

Time From	To	Battery	Target	Rounds	Remarks
8 a		15	Madagascar Tr.	30	Retaliation
8.30 a			"	41	"
11.50	2.30		"	77	"
4.30			Lone Farm	17	Infantry in open
9.30 p		48	AUCHY & DOUVRIN	12	
10 p			Road A29b58 A30		
6.45 a			b 88	15	
7.30			Auchy	15	
7.50			A29 a 7.2 – A29 t 1.2	42	
11.55 a			Madagascar Tr.	12	Parties seen working along trench here. Retaliation
4 p			A22 c 5.7	40	Enemy seen leaving front trench and moving across open to Auchy. On fire being opened they changed direction towards LONE FARM and opened out
7.35 a		17	?	15	Party in open.
1.50 p			House in Auchy A23 c 22	17	
3.15 p			A30 a 9.0	26	House – Suspected O.P.
3.45			Near Diamond Dow Cottage	4	Enemy in open
8.50				7	" "
9 a		9	A22 d 8.5	22	Party carrying timber – dispersed
9.30 a			Z2 trenches	17	Party leaving trench.
11.30 a			Z2 trenches	4	Cooking party.
1 p			A23 a 2.1	20	O.P.
7 p			A24 b 9.7	7	Party.
7.10			A22 a 8.5	5	Party leaving trench.
2.30 p		15	A21 b	24	Working party
11.50 a		50	Embankment Redoubt	5	Work.
9 p	10 p	71	La Bassée – Cauldeux tracks	24	To catch movement.
8	8.30		A16 a 3.4 & Cauldeux	40	Retaliation
2.30 p			A16 d 3.6	24	Suspected O.P. Effective
12.15 a		47	Junction Mud alley – Pekin alley	22	
2.35 p			H6 A29 b	26	O.P.
11.50 a		56	A16 a 29	12	Pump
1.40 p			A6 d 3.2 Battery	25	Ceased fire
3.5 p			Embankment Rd	15	Work

2nd Divisional Artillery

HOSTILE FIRE REPORT.

10th December, 1915.

1 GENERAL INFORMATION.

Battery, at least 4 guns observed on line from BRADDELL Pt (400) over centre of THE THREE CABARETS, firing between 1-15 p.m. and 1-30 p.m. on VERMELLES-HULLUCH road. Presumed H 1 a 7.2. Gun fire was being used. Flashes plainly visible.

Battery located by flash and smoke at A 6 d 3.2 and stopped firing when engaged. It was firing from the ruined houses on the road. It was apparently firing towards FESTUBERT.

2. HOSTILE FIRE.

No.	Time From	To	Nature	Direction from	Area shelled	Remarks.
1.	8-0a		77 mm.	?	Near BRADDELL Pt.	8 Rounds.
2.	8-0a	8-20a	77 mm.	CANTELEUX	A 14 b 9 7	30 Rounds.
3.	8-0a	8-30a	77mm	?	Trs. Zo	
4.	8-30a	8-35a	77mm	?	Front Line CANAL)	20 rounds
5.	9-25a	10-0a	77mm	?	N 1 and GIVENCHY))	30 rounds
6.	10-50a	11-5a	77mm	HAISNES	HOLLOW	
7.	11-15a	11-20a	77mm	,,	,,	
8.	11-50a	12-40p	77mm 105mm	? ?	Trenches Zo	Retaliation to 15th Div.Bombdt. This, as yesterday was pre-arranged.
9.	12-35p		77mm	?	S CAMBRIN	5 rounds.
~~10.~~	~~3-35p~~		~~?~~	~~?~~	~~ANNEQUIN~~	~~? 60 pdr 1 round.~~
10.	3-30p	3-45p	4" gun	LA BASSEE	PONT FIXE	15 rounds, 3 guns in action together.

Major R.A.
Brigade Major R.A.2nd Divn.

1581

DAILY AMMUNITION RETURN

DATE 10 Dec 15

BATTERIES.

Piece	Projectile	Code	50	70	15	48	71	9	16	17	47	56	Total	Per Piece
18-pr	Guns.......													
	Shrapnel...	"A"	44	-	78	126	32	40	21	20	-	-	361	
	H.E.......	"Ax"	5	54	45	47	29	81	-	-	-	-	261	
4.5"	Howitzers..													
	Shrapnel...	"B"									-	-	-	
	H.E.......	"Bx"									1	26	27	

Extract from Progress Report of
1st Battalion Herts. Regt.

Z O was subjected to an intense bombardment at about 10-45 a.m. this morning, apparently as retaliation for recent bombardments. Enemy fired several hundred rounds, including heavies (probably 4 or 5 inch). We asked for artillery assistance and the 15th, 47th (Hows.) and 6 inch replied. At the end of half an hour the enemy were silenced by what appeared to be overwhelming ascendancy.

I cannot speak too highly of the promptitude of 15th Battery.

5-12-1915.
(sd) P.Croft, Lt.Colonel,
Comdg.R.A., 1st Herts. Regt.

(2).

Z Group.

G.O.C., considers this very satisfactory.

R.A., 2nd Divn.
10-12-1915.
Major, R.A.,
Brigade Major, R.A., 2nd Divn.

2nd Divisional Artillery Orders

by

Brigadier-General C.H.SANDERS, D.S.O., Comdg.R.A.,2nd Divn.

10th December,1915.

1174. BRICKS.

Until further orders no bricks are to drawn from stacks at W.21.c.

1175. APPOINTMENT.

No.33742. S.S. H.Handford, 71st Battery, is appointed S.S.Corporal in 34th Brigade, R.F.A., with effect from 8-11-1915 (vice Spillet). He will remain with 36th Brigade until further orders.

L.G.BUXTON, Capt, R.A.

Staff Captain, R.A., 2nd Divn.

R.A. 2 Div. DIARY.

DATE 11.12.15

OBSERVATION CONDITIONS. Observation possible 7.30 am – 4 pm. Light good. Wind S.W. 27 m.h.

WORK DONE BY ENEMY.
What appears to be a new chimney has been started to the right (South) of S⁺ LEONARD church.
Two mounds apparently roofs of Dug outs newly turfed at A.22.d.6.4. One was demolished.

MOVEMENT SEEN.
10.55 am Large party in marching order going along track A.5.a towards VIOLAINES
11 am onwards small parties wearing helmets and packs from trenches towards LES BRIQUES. Total about 150 men.

GUNS LOCATED OR SUSPECTED.

WORKING PARTIES SEEN.
A.16.d.1.0   10 am
A.22.d.3.7   9.30 am party carrying boards

GENERAL.
PEKIN ALLEY seems to be waterlogged.

ACTION.   See over.   Lt. Colonel,
                                    Commanding

ACTION Time		Battery	Target	Rounds	Remarks
From	To				
		Z group			
7.15a		48	Mad Alley	4	Enemy walking outside trench
7.15a		9	A 22 b 9 1½	5	Working party
8 a		9	A 22 c 7 6	12	Movement on road
8.75a		17	A 22 d 7 5	9	Movement
9.15		9	A 22 c 7 6	10	Movement on road
9.15		17	A 22 d 7.5	10	Movement
9.35	10	9	A 22 b 7.8	20	Timber carrying parties
10		9	A 22 c 9.8, 7.7	12	Parties carrying trenches, armed & equipped
11.05		17	Lone Farm & E	9	? movement
11.15		9	A 7 d 4.4 railway	17	movement
12.25		9	A 22 b 9.1	20	Splinter proof Enemy bivac
12.30p		59 Siege	A 22 b 9.9	19	Demolition
2.15p		71	A 28 d 6.4	76	Mound work one demolished
2.30p		48	Dock Alley? Mad alley?	6	movement
3.40			~~A 22 b 9.1 splinter proof~~ A 22 b 7.8	~~10~~	~~good results occupants~~ Timber party
3.15p			Mad alley	11	movement
4.15			Mad alley	2	movement
		A group			
10.15a		16	A 15 d 1.0	14	Work party
11.15a	12	71	A 4 c 2.2 & 1.5a	70	Enemy seen in large
11.15	11.45	50	" "	17	parties moving towards VIOLAINES

2nd Divisional Artillery

HOSTILE FIRE REPORT.

11th December, 1915.

1. GENERAL INFORMATION.

There was a very large fire which started in the enemy's lines about 3-0 p.m. It appeared to be in PONT a VENDIN or LENS.

2 HOSTILE FIRE.

No.	Time From	Time To	Nature	Direction from	Area shelled	Remarks.
	10th.					
1.	7-0p	7-40p	10 cm.	?	PONT FIXE	40 Rounds.
	11th.					
2.	9-30a	9-45a	105 mm.	?	F 29 d	8 Rounds.
3.	11-0a		77 mm.	LA BASSEE	Trenches just N.of CANAL.	40 Rounds.
4.	11-5a		,,	AUCHY.	PONT FIXE & HOLLOW.	20 Rounds.
5.	12-30p	2-10p	5.9"	S.of LA BASSEE.	A 24 a & c	25 Rounds.
6.	12-30p	2-30p	155 mm How.	HAISNES	A 19 b	20 Rounds per hour. No damage.
7.	2-15p	3-45p	77 mm.	?	HARLEY ST A 20 b 4 0	30 Rounds.
8.	2-15p	2-25p	77 mm.	AUCHY.	WOBURN ABBEY	30 Rounds.
9.	2-50p	3-5p	77 mm.	N.of AUCHY	CUINCHY & PONT FIXE	8 Rounds.
10.	2-50p	3-5p		LA BASSEE	Trenches N.of CANAL	30 Rounds.
11.	3-15p	3-45p	4.2" 77 mm.	AUCHY	CUINCHY HOLLOW	50 Rounds.
12.	4-30p		77 mm.	?	A 19 d 6 4	4 Rounds.

Major, R.A.,
Brigade Major, R.A., 2nd Division.

"A" Form.   Army Form C. 2121.
MESSAGES AND SIGNALS.

TO: HQ 1st Corps

Sender's Number: Bm 954
Day of Month: 11
AAA

Particulars of incident yesterday as reported aaa about 2.30pm five rounds fell first four at about 2 minutes interval last round after longer interval aaa One round passed into stable 5th Bde HQ 18 ft above ground hitting two horses and burst 6 ft above ground bursting in open on further side aaa One round hit corner of stable 15 ft above ground and burst in open on further side fragments probably killing two men aaa One round missed corner of stable and entered wall in corner of mining company's yard 4 ft above ground bursting in shed on further side and killing two men aaa last round burst on ground by railings on N side of garden aaa One round not identified aaa All lyddite aaa half of a base and bit of wall of shell picked

"A" Form. Army Form C. 2121.
MESSAGES AND SIGNALS.

up 5" diameter marked R L H aaa cussion fuze picked up defaced no marks discernable aaa Total Damage 4 men killed 2 wounded 2 horses killed aaa

From Ra WW
Time 11 40 am

DAILY AMMUNITION RETURN

DATE 11 Dec 15

BATTERIES.

Piece	Projectile	Code	50	70	15	48	71	9	16	17	47	56	Total	Per Piece
18-pr	Guns......													
	Shrapnel...	"A"	13	45	99	97	42	74	15	76			461	
	H.E.......	"Ax"	4	26	-	32	64	22	-	45			193	
4"	Howitzers..													
	Shrapnel...	"B"									-	-	-	
	H.E.......	"Bx"									56	115	171	

2nd Divisional Artillery Orders

by

Brigadier-General G.H.SANDERS, D.S.O., Comdg.R.A., 2nd Divn.

11th December,15.

1176. SCALES - MATHEMATICAL.

Attention is directed to General Routine Order No.1178 of 27-9-1915. Indents should be submitted to the Ordnance Office as soon as possible.

1177. DIVINE SERVICE.

Divine Service for all R.F.A. units in or near BETHUNE will be held at 9.0 a.m. to-morrow,12th December,1915, in the DIVISIONAL CONCERT HALL, RUE D'AIRE. As many men as possible will attend.

1178. SUPPLIES.

The hour of loading up at Supply Railhead,from 14th instant inclusive,for 2nd Division will be 10-0 a.m.

L.G.BUXTON, Capt, R.A.

Staff Captain, R.A., 2nd Divn.

DIARY

2nd Div. RA

DATE

12.12.15

1588

OBSERVATION CONDITIONS.
Observation possible 7.15 am to 3.45 pm. Light v.g. 10.45 – 1.45. Some showers. Wind N.W. slight.

WORK DONE BY ENEMY.
New work has been constructed on S.W. outskirts of VIOLAINES. Some work has been done behind LONE FARM northwards.

MOVEMENT SEEN.
Enemy again seen at intervals in morning walking in open A10b 10.3. Ten men were seen 7.15 am at A16 2.9. At Z point fewer were seen.

GUNS LOCATED OR SUSPECTED.
Flash of 77 mm guns bearing 88° true from Boyau 9 at 3.30 pm firing on A 27 d. Flash to burst 9 secs. Probably A 30 b 7.5

WORKING PARTIES SEEN.
10.20 am A16 b 2.1
10.30   A16 d 3.1 behind trucks
1 pm   A 22 a 10.8 party carrying wood. Disappeared behind A brickstack.

GENERAL.
Several mounds have become visible, showing up greener than their surroundings – two by MAD POINT and four near LES BRIQUES. Some work has been done on the last – sandbags visible.

OP in Auchy A22d 9.5 has been hit several times, and heavy timber work laid bare. More treatment needed.

Enemy opened a bombardment on Z0 at 2.50 pm and continued for 20 minutes.

ACTION.   See over.

Lt. Colonel
Commanding

ACTION Thiepval					
From	To	Battery	Target	Rounds	Remarks
		Z group			
7.20		17	Nr Lone Farm	20	work party
7.20		9	A22b78	15	Timber carrying
8.20		47	A29a94	10	work party
9.20	9.50	9	A29b37	19	work parties
10.20		9	A22b75	12	Timber carrying
10		17	Lone Farm	3	work party
12.30p		5 siege	A22d8.8	35	Demolition of O.P.
1.15		48	Mounds near Les Briques	21	One large hole in one roof
2	3.15		A22d96 H0	59	Several good hits - see above
3.10p			Lone Farm + Nr	16	work party
4 pm	4.25		A23a0.5	29	Men leaving trenches
		A group			
7.15		71	A16d8.9	25	movement
10.10	11	71	A15d9.9	45	New Snipers post destroyed
10.30	10.55	56	New work W. Edge S VIOLAINES	20	
10.30	12.30	50	A10b10.5	25	movement
11	11.30	16	A16d3.0	12	movement behind trees
11.10		16	A brickstack	7	Man working in pink Sou'wester
1		15	A22a10.8	6	wood carrying

Group Diary

Date — DEC 12TH 1915

General

Observation possible 7.15 AM to 3.45 PM
Light very good 10.45 - 1.45 After that showery.
Wind NW Moderate.

Enemy were again seen at intervals during the forenoon walking in the open A10 b 10.3 and engaged by 50TH Battery. Another party of about 10 men were seen at 7.15 AM walking in open A16 d 8.9 and were fired on by 71 Battery.

Enemy's Works

Working Parties 10.20 AM A16 b 2.1
   11.30 AM working behind trucks A16 d 3.0 - 3.1
   1 PM Fatigue party carrying wood A 22 a 10.8 disappeared behind A Brickstack.

The enemy has apparently been constructing a new work on the S. Western outskirts of VIOLAINES.

Action

No	Time From	Time To	Battery	Target	Rounds	Remarks
(1)	7.15		71	A 16 d 8.9	25	a few of the enemy crossing in the open
(2)	10.10 A	11 A M	71	A 15 d 9.9	45	New Snipers post destroyed
(3)	10.30	10.55	56	New work on Western Edge of VIOLAINES	20	
(4)	10.30	12.30	50	Enemy seen at intervals at A 10 b 10.5	25	
(5)	11 A	11.30	16	A 16 d 3.0	12	Movement behind trucks
(6)	11.10		16	Right corner A Brickstack	7	Men seen working in pinks SOU'WESTER
(7)	11.35		71	A 16 a	30	Retaliation
(8)	11.35	12.8	56 & 50	CULVERT & EMBANKMENT REDOUBT	15 & 20	"
(9)	12.30		59 S	A 22 d 8.8	35	Demolition
(10)	1 PM		16	A 22 a 10.8	6	Party carrying wood
(11)	1.45 PM		71	A 16 a	30	Retaliation
(12)	3 PM		56	A 12 d 5.0 House	21	"
(13)	4.15		56	CANAL HOUSE	9	"

B. Quiller Couch Lieut & Adjt
for Lt Col. R.F.A.
Gordg A Group

Z GROUP DIARY.

B.

DATE - 12-12-15

General.
A curious number of green mounds are now visible from O.B. especially noticeable are two where there ought to be no grass: near MAD point. The green is also very strikingly vivid. There are two near Mad point, two near Les briques and two more near the last two. The "haystack" near Lone farm is also growing green. A lot of work has been done near the last and many sand bags are visible. ~~Inem y's Works~~. Zo was subjected to 30 mm (civ) bombardment at 2.50 pm but this did not appear so intense as recently.

Not reported on Form A. Flash of 77mm gun or guns firing on A.27.d 3.~~35~~ pm. bearing 88° true from O.B in Boyau 9. It was made out to be at A.30 b 7.5. Time between flash and burst 9 sec.

Observation possible 7.15 am.
Not so many germans seen today.

Action.
over.

No.	Time. From.	To.	Battery.	Target.	Rounds.	Remarks.
1	7.30 am		9th Batt	A 22 b 7.8	15	partz carrying timber.
2	9.20 am	9.50 am		A 29 b 3.7	19	disp. working parties
3	10.30 am			A 22 b 7.5	12	partz carrying timber.
4	2 pm	3.15 pm		Houses in Auchy A 22 D 9.6	69	see report above.
5	4 pm	4.25 pm		A 23 a 0.5	29	men leaving trenches
6	2.20 pm		15th Batt	New trenches.	4	retaliation
7	2.45 pm	3.15 pm		" Madagascar	145	"
8	3.20 pm			Haisnes	12	"
9	4.30 pm			Vicinity Lone farm	5	to catch reliefs.
10	8.20 am			A 29 a 9.4	10	working partz
11	10.55 am			Haisnes + roads Junc. Petri + Mad ally	21	Aeroplane reg.
12	2.20 pm			Auchy	33	retaliation

Lieut.Colonel.
Commanding Group.

Work has been done behind Lone farm Northwards.

9th Batt fired on an OB in Auchy A22d96. Suspicions were aroused by loopholes in the roof. After several hits wooden structure was disclosed with extremely stout beams which were meant to carry more than a mere floor. Treatment to be continued.

No.	Time		Batt	Location	Rounds	Remarks
13	7.20 am	×	17th Batt	Open space in Transvaal and near Lone farm	20	wasp nests
14	5.10 am	×		Lone farm	3	"
15	2.6 pm			Place where party emerged in No 14	3	registration
16	3.30 pm	×		Work behind Lone farm	16	
17	7.30 pm to 7.30 am		48th Batt and 71st ×	Haines Donovin Road	22	
18	10.30 pm		"	Petrin alley, Mad alley, Dooh alley, Chateau alley	9	
19	9.50 am			Dooh alley	2	2 germans
20	10.50 am			"	5	"
21	11.5 am			Pope's nose	5	retaliation
22	11.25 am			Dooh alley	3	"
23	11.40 am 12 noon			Trench in front of 3 Cabarets	10	registration
24	12 noon 12.5 pm			Petrin alley	4	"
25	1.15 pm	×		Green mounds near Auchy	21	one large hole in one roof.
26	1.45 pm			Auchy	14	various
27	3. pm			Railway trench	40	retaliation
28	3.30 pm – 3.45 pm			Guns A30b7.5	35	—
29	12.30 pm	×	5 9th siege	A22d88	35	demolition of OB

Rodd
Adj: 41st Bde

2nd Divisional Artillery

HOSTILE   FIRE   REPORT.

12th December, 1915.

HOSTILE FIRE.

No.	Time From	To	Nature	Direction From	Area Shelled	Remarks.
1.	11-5 a	--	77mm	A U C H Y	SIMS Keep & vicinity	6 rounds (2 air)
2.	11-25a	11-29a	4.2"	S.LA BASSEE	(PONT FIXE & CHEYNE WALK	42 rounds
3.	11-50a	12-50p				3-gun Battery.
4.	1-35p	1-45p				
5.	3-50p	3-55p				
6.	1-45p	2-30p	77mm & 4.2"	?	GUNNER SIDING	20 rounds 15 ,,
7.	2-35p	--	105 mm G U N.	?	17th Battery	3 rounds (2 air) H. E.
8.	2-45p	3-15p	155mm 77mm	?	S.Vermelles Rd.	200 rounds in bursts.

Major R.A.
Brigade Major R.A. 2nd Divn.

T590

DAILY AMMUNITION RETURN

DATE 12 Dec 15

BATTERIES.

Piece	Projectile	Code	50	70	15	48	71	9	16	17	47	56	Total	Per Piece
18-pr	Guns......													
	Shrapnel...	"A"	96	49	21	77	57	93	53	23			469	
	H.E.......	"Ax"	4	105	7	48	63	82	6	17			332	
4.5"	Howitzers..													
	Shrapnel...	"B"										66	66	
	H.E.......	"Bx"									22	126	148	

R.A.2nd Divn.Inst/50.

SUBJECT - 1st Corps Defence Scheme - Artillery.

A Group.
Z Group.
59th Siege Bty.
44th Brigade.
34th Brigade.(For information).

    Herewith a copy of the scheme for defence of VILLAGE, LE TOURET and ESSARS Lines, which has been submitted to 1st Corps for approval.

2. It has been suggested that the Village Line positions be constructed, but that the positions further to the rear be not constructed on account of the rapid decay of materials.

3. 1st Corps direct that divisions undertake no work in rear until the present firing positions are in every way complete, and define a complete position as follows :-

    (a) Headcover for all guns and dug-outs 4.2 in.howitzer proof. (This applies to 6" howitzers).

    (b) Observation Stations complete as regards protection, comfort and sanitation.

    (c) Detachment billets made as comfortable and sanitary as possible.

4. This work will be carried on as necessary, and a report will be made as each position is complete. If material is not made available by the R.E.Companies in the sections report should be made to R.A., H.Q. When iron rails are not available for roofing, 3" x 9" timbers will be demanded.

5. Groups will arrange to patrol regularly any alternative and Village Line positions. 44th Brigade H.Q. will take charge of Le Touret Line positions.

6. Positions not occupied,on which any work has been done, will be marked at each end with a board having a stencilled or painted notice -

    Artillery Position No. -

    Not to be damaged.

    Numbers will be allotted as soon as the scheme is approved by 1st Corps.

7. Any changes in the scheme desired by Group Commanders should be reported.

R.A., 2nd Divn.
12-12-1915.

                 Major, R.A.,
Brigade Major, R.A., 2nd Divn.

SOUTHERN Division.

Village Line.

No.	POSITION.	ALTERNATIVE	FOR GUNS	TO FIRE ON	OBSERVING STATIONS	STATE OF PREPARATION.
	F 23 b 5 5 (F)	F 29 b 9 3 (B)	6 18-pr.	A 26 d	Four hundred(A) or The Ruin (D)	(A) Completed
	F 23 c 6 2 (D)	F 29 a 9 8 (B)	6 18-pr.	A 26 b	Four hundred2(A) or The Ruins2(D)	(B) Not begun.
	F 23 a 1 7 (F)	F 29 b 9 6 (B)	6 18-pr.	A 26 b	Braddell Castle 1(A) or The Babe(A)	(C) Occupied by civilians.
	F 24 a 4 8 (A)		3 18-pr.	A 21 c	Wilsons Ho.(A) or The Babe.	(D) Under construction.
	F 23 d 10 9 (A)	F 23 b 6 8	5 18-pr.	A 21 a	A 20 c 2 4 Ho.(C)	(E) Under reconstruction
	F 17 a 2 2 (E)	F 17 c 0 4 (B)	6 18-pr.	A 15 c	Ho. A 14 c 5 8(B)	(F) Occupied by heavies.
	F 32 b 5 1 (B)		3 18-pr.	A 15 a	A 13 b 7 2 truck	
	Reserve		3 18-pr.			
	F 30 c 2 4 (D)	F 30 c 6 2 (A)	3 4.5How.	A 27	Tower of Babel(A) or Ridge Ho. (A)	
	F 23 b 3 6 (E)	F 23 a 6 5 (B)	6 4.5How.	A 21 A 15	A 20 c 4 9 (B). A 19 d 9 6 (C). Ho.	
	F 30 c 8 8 (A)	F 10 d 7 2 (B)	4 6in. How.	A 15 A 27	Tower of Babel(A) or Greenwoods Ho. (A).	

SOUTHERN Division.

LE TOURET LINE.

No.	POSITION	ALTERNATIVE	FOR GUNS	TO FIRE ON	OBSERVING STATIONS	STATE OF PREPARATION
1	L 2 a 2 6 (B)	F 23 c 7 2 (B)	6 18-pr.	F 22 F 17	F 20 d Ho.(C)	(A) Completed.
2	F 14 b 8 4 (A)	F 14 a 0 2 (B)	6 18-pr.	F 11 c 17	a F 10 d 10 7(A) or d Ho.(C)	(B) Not begun.
3	F 7 a 8 4 (B)	F 7 a 1 2 (B)	3 18-pr.	F 17 a 2 c	F 10 d 10 7 d 6(A) or F 10 d 8 3Ho(C)	(C) Occupied by civilians.
4	F 13 d 7 9 (B)	F 13 c 1 7(B)	3 13-pr.	F 23	F 20 a Ho.(C) or F 13 c 3 2 d.o(B)	
5	F 13 b 9 1(B)	F 7 a 2 4 (B)	6 18-pr.	F 23 F 22	F 20 a Mo(C) or F 13 c 3 2 d.o(B)	
6	F 8 d 2 7 (A)	F 13 a 2 1(B)	6 18-pr.	F 23	F 21 d d.o(A) or F 21 a Ho.(C)	
7	Reserve.		3 18-pr.			
8	Reserve.		3 18-pr.			
9	F 18 d 7 7(B)	F 14 c 4 7(B)	6 4.5How	F 23 F 28	Ho.F 14 c(C) or F 13 c 3 2 d.o(B)	
10	F 14 a 4 4(B)	F 13 a 2 6(B)	6 4.5How	F 11 F 15	Ho.F 10 d(C)	
11	F 8 c 8 0 (B)	F 14 a 3 8(B)	4 6 in.	F 17 F 23	(Ho.F 14 c(C) or (F 13 c 3 2 d.o(B) (Ho.F 10 d(C)	

SOUTHERN Division.

ESSARS LINE.

No.	POSITION.	ALTERNATIVE.	FOR GUNS.	TO FIRE ON.	OBSERVING STATIONS.	STATE OF PREPARATION.
	F 22 d 8 8(B)		6 18-pr.	F 19	F 13 c / d o (B)	(B) Not begun.
	F 22 b 2 1(B)		6 18-pr.	F 19 F 20	do	(O) Occupied by inhabitants
	F 23 a 0 4(B)		3 18-pr.	F 20 F 21	do	
	F 17 b 4 3(B)		4 18-pr.	F 15 d, F 21 b	F 14 c Ho.(C)	
	F 7 a 1 2(B)		3 18-pt.	F 10 c, F 18 a	F 14 b Ho.(C)	
	F 7 a 2 4(B)		6 18-pr.	F 16 a, F 15 d	F 14 b Ho.(C)	
	Reserve.		6 18-pr.	–		
	Reserve.		6 18-pr.	–		
	F 18 d 7 7(B)		3 4.5"	F 19 20 21	F 13 c do(B)	
	F 13 a 2 3(B)		6 4.5"	F 10 18	F 14 b Ho.(C)	
	F 7 c 6 2(B)		4 6in.	F 10 21	F 13 c do(B) / H 14 b Ho.(C)	

— SKETCH SHOWING —
— LINES REFERRED TO —

SCALE 1/40,000

Northern Division

Southern Division

IV Corps

Front line
Village line
Le Touret line
Tissues System

R.A., 2nd DIVISION SITUATION. - 12-12-1915.

GROUP	UNIT	BATTERY POSITION	WAGON LINE
-	34th Brigade H.Q.		BETHUNE (Rue St.Pry).
A.	50th Battery.	F 18 a 3 2	F 13 c 9 9
A	70th Battery.	F 24 c 8 4	F 13 c 9 9
A	36th Brigade H.Q.	A 19 d 3 2	
Z	15th Battery	G 8 a 0 5	F 14 a 5 2
Z	48th Battery	A 25 b 1 0	F 14 a 5 2
A	71st Battery	F 18 a 8 8 (4)	E 5 a 5 10
A		E 8 c (1)	
Z		A 14 c 2 6 (1)	
●	41st Brigade H.Q.	A 19 d 5 3	
Z	9th Battery	F 18 c 3 1	F 7 a 7 8
H.A.	16th Battery	F 24 c 9 2	W 26 b 3 3
Z	17th Battery	F 24 a 8 2	F 13 d 2 10
-	44th Brigade H.Q.		BETHUNE
●	47th Battery	F 30 c 7 2	W 21 c 9 2
A	56th Battery	A 20 a 5 2	CHAMP DE MARS
-	59th Siege Battery	F 30 c 5 6	- -
-	34th B.A.C.		E 18 b
-	36th B.A.C.		W 29 b 8 5
-	41st B.A.C.		E 18 b 9 3
-	44th B.A.C.		CHAMP DE MARS
-	D.A.C.		E 21 a

2nd Divisional Artillery Orders

by

Brigadier-General G.H.SANDERS, D.S.O.,Comdg.R.A,2nd Divn.

<u>12th December,1915.</u>

<u>1179. HEADCOVER.</u>

Reference R.A.Order No.1171, dated 8-12-1915.
Units requiring poles and brushwood can draw as many wagon loads as they require on obtaining a chit from this Office.

L.G.BUXTON,Capt,R.A.

Staff Captain,R.A.,2nd Divn.

R.A. 2nd Div. DIARY

DATE 13 Dec 1915

OBSERVATION CONDITIONS. 7.15 am till 11.30 am poor, to 3.55 pm
~~fair~~ good. Wind N. to WNW 20 m.p.h.

WORK DONE BY ENEMY. Some work has been done about A 29 a 1.2.
A new mound of white chalky earth has been
thrown up near Mad Point.

MOVEMENT SEEN. ~~Little~~ movement seen. Only 2 - 4 men moving at intervals
in A section. In Z Section one party of 30 men moved along road
A 29 b 28 - A 29 d 28. M.G. turned S.[?] fire on them. Further movement
of small numbers at a run were seen at same places.

GUNS LOCATED OR SUSPECTED.

As reported in hostile fire report.

WORKING PARTIES SEEN. A 15 d 9.0 digging   A 16 d 7.0   8.15 am
                      A 22 d 8.8   " on road.   A 15 d 9.0   11 am
                      Zz point trench (very energetic)
                      Scams line trench guns shell - Boy a 21.

GENERAL. Pook Alley seems very wet from movement in open.
There is a rope hanging from a chimney A 24 d 7.7.
When our guns shelled Haisnes today a light was seen
flashing from a house in the direction of A 23 b 9.2.
Enemy's activity confined to somewhat heavy shelling
of PONT FIXE with 4.2 howitzers all day.
Small minenwerfer active at A brickstack 8.7 & 12.7
pm. ceased on 56th firing.
Trench A 16 a 2.7 seems to be in good order from pace
enemy can carry planks along it.

ACTION.   See over.   Lt. Colonel,
                                      Commanding

ACTION Time From	To	Battery (Principal)	Target	Rounds	Remarks
11 am	11.45	9	Ho. A23a1.3	79	Inspected O.P.
7 p		9	A22d9.6 Ho	45	Fortified Ho.
11 a		17	A29a1.2	13	New work.
7.25	8.30	48	A29b2.4		
1.30 p		48	A29d28 Les Briques mounds	40 6	Movement.
1.25 p	1.75	47	A28b x6	4	Working party
4.05	5.5	47	Pekin alley and alley junct.	12	Watch for bomb Stokes
8.30	.3	59 Siege	A22d8.8	54	O.B. destroyed.
8.7 p	15th	56	A Mickstack	13	Minenwerfer silenced.
10.15 a 13th		56	A18a1.1	31	Battery.

DIARY

DATE DEC 13TH 1915

OBSERVATION CONDITIONS. Observation possible 7.30 AM – 3.55 PM Wind N.N.W Moderate Light good all day

WORK DONE BY ENEMY. "NIL"

MOVEMENT SEEN.
- 10 AM — 4 men seen S.W of CANTELEUX
- 7.50 AM — 3 " " A 16 b 5.5
- 10 AM — 2 " " A 11 c 3.3
- 1 PM — 5 " " A 10 a 5.2
- 2 PM — 3 " " A 16 a 2.7 to 2.9
- 2.30 PM — 6 " " A 16 c 2.0

GUNS LOCATED OR SUSPECTED.

From A 15 C 1.7 Flashes and smoke from guns clearly visible at 10.15 AM A 18 a 1.1 and 3.20 PM A 6 d 3.2. Bearings to these Batteries have often been taken and always confirm position as seen from HUN VIEW. A cross bearing is badly wanted

WORKING PARTIES SEEN.
- 8.15 AM — A 16 d 7.0
- 11 AM — A 15 d 9.0

GENERAL. The enemy's artillery activity has again been confined to somewhat heavy shelling of PONT FIXE throughout the day with 4.2 HOWS. As formed bodies of Infantry use the N Tow Path of CANAL east of PONT FIXE in good daylight this is hardly to be wondered at.

MINNENWERFER small were active at 8.7 PM and 12.7 PM apparently firing from A Brickstack they stopped when engaged by 56 HOW Battery. From the pace enemy were able to carry planks along trench A 16 a 2.7 they would appear to be in good repair

B Quiller Couch
Lieut & Acty
for Lt.Colonel,
Commanding A Group

ACTION. See over.

ACTION

Time From	To	Battery	Target	Rounds	Remarks
7.30 P		16	A 16 d 3.1	6	Saloo. Infantry reported work
8.7 P		56	A Brickstack	13	MINENWERFER.
7.30 A		71	A 16 b 5.5	8	Movement.
10 A		71	A 11 c 3.3	9	"
9.30 A	10 A	71	A 12 d 7.1	35	Retaliation
10.15 A		56	A 18 a 1.1	31	Battery.
10.47		50	A 12 d 7.1	9	Retaliation
11.15		50	EMBANKMENT REDOUBT.	10	"
11.8 AM		71	A 16 c 1.9	25	"
11.30		59 S	A 22 c 8.8	17	Demolition.
12.7 PM		56	A Brickstack	31	Trench Mortar.
2.30		71	A 17 a 5.5	30	Retaliation
"		16	A 16 c 2.0	4	Movement
2.35		59 S	A 16 c 4.½	7	Demolition.
2.55		50	EMBANKMENT REDOUBT	12	Retaliation.
3. PM		16	A 22 b 9.7	4	"
"		59 S	A 22 d 10.7½	37	Demolition
3.15		16	AUCHY X roads A 22 b 10.9	4	Retaliation
3.20		56	A 16 d 3.2	7	Battery at once ceased firing.
5 PM		59 S	A 28 b 8.3	8	Retaliation.

Z group DIARY.

DATE 13-12-15

OBSERVATION CONDITIONS. Observation possible at 7.15 am but poor till 11.30 am when it improved somewhat.

WORK DONE BY ENEMY. Some work has been done about A 29 a 1.21 A new mound of white chalky earth has been thrown up near Mad pt.

MOVEMENT SEEN. Not so much movement today. Two men walked up from Auchy to support line and were hidden by craters in Z2 & A1. They did not seem to enjoy their walk especially the end of it. They were carrying canteens.
Movement was seen on railway in front of Les Briques. Some guns are now laid on this
continued below:-

GUNS LOCATED OR SUSPECTED.

NIL.
SUSPECTED: behind HAISNES ridge in vicinity of A 30 d.

WORKING PARTIES SEEN. at A15 d 9.0 digging. at A22 d 8.8 on road digging.
A very energetic party was reported in front tr. of Z 2 South at 9.30 am
Another equally energetic party was reported in second line tr. between Gun St. & Boy an 21

GENERAL. A rope can be seen hanging from a chimney in A 24 d 7.7.
When our guns were shelling HAISNES this morning a light was seen flashing from a house in the direction of A 23 b 9.2 (from Tower of Babel)

About 30 Germans were were seen walking along road A 29 b 2.4 to A 29 d 2.8. These were fired on. A few minutes later parties of three were seen crossing at a fast run. The fire seemed effective.
Some few were again seen walking along top of Dook alley. It would appear Dook alley is very wet.

ACTION.   See over.

Rodd
Lt. Colonel,
Adjutant
Commanding Z group.

ACTION

Time From	To	Battery	Target	Rounds	Remarks
10.30am		9th Batt	Working party	25	on road A22 b 8 8
11.am	11.45am		House A 23a 1.3	79	suspected O.B.
12 noon			A 29 b 4.7	15	working parties
2 pm			A22d 9.6 house	45	fortified house
3.30pm			2nd line to	12	energetic party
9.30 am		15th Batt	Madagascar tr	4	retaliation
9.45 am			Madagascar tr.	18	"
4.45 pm			" + vicinity	25	" to bombardment
11.0 am		17th Batt	Some new work	13	A29a 1.21
12.5 pm			Trenches	19	
12.30 pm			Movement observed	10	
2.4 pm			Trenches	7	retaliation
2.20 pm			"	22	
2.25.4 pm			" + work	30	
9 pm 12/12/15		48th Batt	Night lines	6	
7.25 am	8.30am		Germans on road A29 b 2.4 to A29 d 2.8	40	as reported over leaf.
9.45 am			Trenches	14	retaliation
11.15 am			Germans on top of Dook ally	2	2 germans, missed the green ones.
1.30 pm			Les Bougues mermob	6	
3.10pm			Houses Auchy	10	O.B.
10.10am	11am	47th Batt	Houses + roads	5	retaliation.
12.5 pm	12.75 pm		Trench A28 b 2.6	14	working party disp.
2.37pm	3.20pm		Suspects in Auchy	29	
4.45pm	5.57pm		Junct. Petrin + Mad alley		retaliation to bomb. ZO
			Branch keep	12	
7.30pm 12/12/15		71? gun	Auchy	12	
7.45 am			Railway to Madagascar tr.	12	
11.30 am		59th Siege	A22d 8.8 house	17	to destroy O.B. It was destroyed
2.35 pm			A 16 C 4.7	7	registration
3.0 pm			A22d 8.8 house	37	
4.45 pm			A28 b 8.3	8	retaliation to shelling ZO.

2nd Divisional Artillery

HOSTILE FIRE REPORT.

13th December, 1915.

1. GENERAL INFORMATION.

Batteries located A 18 a 1.1 and A 6 d 3.2 were again active at 10-15 a.m. and 3-20 p.m. respectively. The flashes are clearly visible from A 15 c 1.7. The smoke of the guns can clearly be seen bearings taken from here on several occasions give the same position.

2 HOSTILE FIRE.

No.	Time From	Time To	Nature	Direction from	Area Shelled	Remarks.
1	9-30a	10-0a	4.2"	HAISNES	PONT FIXE	40 rounds
2	9-45a		77mm	AUCHY	Z o	12 ,,
3	10-45a	11-0a	4.2"	HAISNES	PONT FIXE	14 ,,
4	12-45p		4.2" (Air)	AUCHY	Z1	1 "Wooley"
5	1-0p		4.2"	?	GIVENCHY	12 rounds
6	2-55p		4.2"	?	A 21 b 5.3	
7	3-0p	3-5p	77mm	LA BASSEE	HOLLOW	7 rounds
8	3-5p	3-20p	4.2" 77mm	HAISNES ?	PONT FIXE ,,	12 ,, 10 ,,
9	3-15p		4.2" (Air)	AUCHY	200X E of 48th By.	2 ,,
10	4-35p		77mm 4.2"	?	Z o	Short Bombardment.

for Major R.A.

Brigade Major R.A. 2nd Dn.

7597

DAILY AMMUNITION RETURN

DATE 13 Dec 15

BATTERIES.

Piece	Projectile	Code	50	70	15	48	71	9	16	17	47	56	Total Per Piece
18-pr	Guns......												
	Shrapnel...	"A"	41	32	192	96	5	30	41	34	—	—	471
	H. E.......	"Ax"	5	63	16	46	140	162	4	26	—	—	462
4.5"	Howitzers..												
	Shrapnel...	"B"									—	—	—
	H. E.......	"Bx"									42	126	168

2nd Divisional Artillery Orders

by

Brigadier-General G.H.SANDERS, D.S.O., Comdg.R.A.,2nd Divn.

13th December,1915.

1180. REFILLING.

From 14th instant inclusive lorries will arrive at refilling point at 8-30 a.m. and supply wagons at 9-0 a.m.

1181. RETURNS.

All units will report to this office by midday 15th inst. the number of Church of England Officers and O.Ranks under their command.

1181. HEADCOVER.

Reference R.A.Orders Nos. 1171 & 1179, dated 8th Decr, and 12th Decr,1915 respectively.
The 47th Battery have moved from W.21.c, but the poles and brushwood will still be issued from this place. A N.C.O. of the 47th Battery will be there and will issue poles and brushwood against chits signed in this Office.

1182. RETURNS - EVACUATION

Veterinary cases should not be included in return of horses proposed for casting by D.D.R.
Unless cases of debility are attributed to old age they should not be included.

1183. FOOTBALL TOURNAMENT.

Lieut.Dunlop, A.V.C., has been selected to represent R.A. 2nd Division on the Divisional Football Committee.
Os.C.Brigades and D.A.C. are requested to send a representative to meet this officer at 34th B.A.C.,E.18.b.5.5, at 3-0 p.m. on Wednesday 15th December,1915.

L.G.BUXTON, Capt, R.A.
Staff Captain, R.A., 2nd Divn.

2nd Div

DIARY

DATE

OBSERVATION CONDITIONS. Observation possible 9.45 am to 4 pm. Wind WSW. Light good 12.30 to 2, otherwise bad.

WORK DONE BY ENEMY.
New dug outs at A.17.a.5.8 (apparently)
New work A.16.c.1.9, nature not reported

MOVEMENT SEEN.
1. Germans seen entering mounds A.22.d.8.6
2. In open space A.22.b.8.7 - A.22.b.9.8½
3. 7 men running across open A.10.a.3.3

GUNS LOCATED OR SUSPECTED.
nil

WORKING PARTIES SEEN. A.29.a.2.1
A.21.b.9½.2 - A.21.b.7½.2 10.15 pm (infantry report)
A.16.d.2.1 10.15 am
Sunken Road redoubt 2.30 & 4 pm

GENERAL.
Enemy quiet all day.
Hostile aeroplane up 10 - 10.30 am
Three white wooden Crosses have been put up in the wire in front of PEKIN TRENCH.

ACTION. See over.
No action of importance. Movement fired on.

Lt. Colonel
Commanding

ACTION Time		Battery	Target	Rounds	Remarks
From	To				

ACTION Time		Battery	Target	Rounds	Remarks
From	To				

ACTION Time		Battery	Target	Rounds	Remarks
From	To				
10.45 P		16	A 21 b 9½ 2 to 7½ 2	12	Working Party
8.15		71	A 10 a 3.3	10	Enemy seen
10.15 A		16	A 16 d 2.1	6	Working party
"		50	NE Brickstacks	20	Fires very active
11 AM		56	" "	19	Retaliation
11.30		71	A 17 a 6.7	15	"
"		16	2nd line N of LA BASSÉE Rd	24	"
12.13		71	New work A16c19	30	
2.10		16	A 21 b 7.7	7	Trench mortar with large puff of white smoke
2.5	2.30	56	A 17 a 6.7 & CANAL HOUSE	38	Retaliation
2	3	50	EMBANKMENT REDOUBT	70	Considerable damage to parapet
2.45		56	Retaliated on enemy 2nd line opposite A2	3	Trench Mortar
"		16	A 21 b 7.7	6	Trench Mortar
2.20		71	A 16 a 2.1 - 0.5	35	
4		50	EMBANKMENT REDOUBT	20	Enemy seen digging

DIARY.

DATE DEC 14 1915

OBSERVATION CONDITIONS. Observation possible 9.45 AM to 4 PM. Wind SSW very light in morning but increasing all day. Light good 12 noon to 3 PM.

WORK DONE BY ENEMY. Enemy have done some work on what appear to be new dug outs A 17 a 5.8. There is a new work A 16 c 1.9.

MOVEMENT SEEN. Enemy were seen at 11.30 A.M in open between Houses A 22 b 9.7 – A 22 b 9.8½
At 8.15 AM 7 Germans seen running across open A 10 a 8.3

GUNS LOCATED OR SUSPECTED. NIL

WORKING PARTIES SEEN.
10.15 PM A 21 b 9½.2 – A 21 b 7½.2 as reported by Infantry.
10.15 AM A 16 d 2.1
2.30 PM EMBANKMENT REDOUBT

GENERAL. The Enemy have been quiet all day. Hostile Aeroplane over German lines 10 AM to 10.30 AM.

B Quiller Couch
Lieut & Adjt
for

ACTION. See over.

Lt. Colonel,
Commanding "A" Group

ACTION Time From	To	Battery	Target	Rounds	Remarks.
11.20am	11.30am	9th Bat	A23a58	20	Retaliation
5pm	13/12/15	15th Bat	Madagascar	18	by request of inf.
3.15pm	14th	—	Lone farm	6	
9.30am		17th Bat	Men in open	2	
11.30am	12.43pm		Suspected house	52	Auchy
2.40pm	3.20pm		Trenches	20	Instruction of E A officers
3.20pm			Wire on POPE'S Nose	17	registration
2.20pm	2.30pm	47th	Haisnes X roads	10	Aeroplane registration
3.5pm	3.20pm		A28b.2.6	5	working party
3am	3.5am	48th Batt	Front tr. Chateau alley	6	
8.15am			"	2	to stop fire on aeroplane
10.30am	11.48am		" + C.T.	24	retaliation
2.30pm			"	8	registration for W.C.
4.30pm	4.35pm		"	4	retaliation
10.30pm	13/12/15	71st gun	Haisnes Auchy rd.	18	
		59th Siege did not fire.			

Rodd
Adj Z group

DIARY.   Z group.

DATE 14-12-15.

OBSERVATION CONDITIONS. Bad, except between 12.30 and 2 p.m.
Extremely bad for long distance observation.
It became possible on front line at 8 a.m.

WORK DONE BY ENEMY.

MOVEMENT SEEN. Germans were seen entering the grass
Thomas A 22 d 8.6. Some Germans were also seen
in open space between A 22 b 8.7 and A 22 b 9.8½.
A German was seen in the front line with a heavy maul
A 21 d 6.4

GUNS LOCATED OR SUSPECTED.

WORKING PARTIES SEEN. A party was seen about A 29 a 2.1

GENERAL.
Three white wooden crosses have been erected in
the wire in front of PEKIN trench.

ACTION.   See over.   Lt. Colonel,
                                         Commanding

2nd Divisional Artillery
HOSTILE FIRE REPORT.

14th December, 1915.

No.	HOSTILE FIRE Time From	To	Nature	Direction from	Area shelled	Remarks
1	9-58a	10-0a	77mm	?	A 15 b 4.2	
2	10-30a		4.2"	?	ditto	
3	10-30a		77mm	HAISNES	Z1 trenches	3 rounds
4	11-4a	11-30a	105mm	?	A 20 d. A 27a	20 ,,
5	11-15a	11-25a	4.2"	?	HARLEY ST.	
6	11-30a	11-37a	77mm	LA BASSEE	GUNNER SIDING	
7	11-30a	11-35a	77mm	?	A 21 b	8 rounds
8	11-32a		77mm	A U C H Y	GUNNER SIDING	
9	11-37a	11-45a	77mm	?	Zo	20 rounds
10	12-15p		105mm 77mm	A U C H Y	S. of COWL He	
11	2-1p	2-17p	77mm	do	A 15 b CUINCHY	
12	2-15p	2-50p	4.2"	HAISNES ~~HAISNES~~	HOLLOW	
13	2-20p	2-55p	77mm 105mm	A U C H Y HAISNES	Zo	Fairly heavy Bombardment.
14	2-45p	3-10p	4.2"	HAISNES	Front line by N 1.	

Major, R.A.,
Brigade Major, R.A., 2nd Divn.

DAILY AMMUNITION RETURN

DATE

BATTERIES.

Piece	Projectile	Code	50	70	15	48	71	9	16	17	47	56	Total	Per Piece
18-pr	Guns......													
	Shrapnel...	"A"	84	50	18	68	26	79	40	59	–	–	424	
	H. E.......	"Ax"	15	6	–	26	73	126	14	52	–	–	312	
4.5"	Howitzers..													
	Shrapnel...	"B"									–	–	–	
	H. E.......	"Bx"									60	130	190	

SECRET

COPY No. 12.

2nd Divisional Artillery Operation Order No.10.

14th December, 1915.

Reference Sheet 36c N.W.1. $\frac{1}{10,000}$

1. Provided the weather conditions permit operations will be carried out on 15th December and night 15th/16th December with the object of:-
    (a) Destroying hostile mine shafts and parapets.
    (b) Causing loss to the enemy.
    (c) Obtaining identifications and prisoners.
    (d) Obtaining information regarding enemy's trenches.
    (e) Lowering the enemy's moral.

2. The operations will comprise:-
    (i) A bombardment lasting approximately 4 hours, probably 10-0 a.m. to 2-0 p.m.
    (ii) An attack by gas during the hours of darkness, followed by
    (iii) Incursions of 6 small parties into the enemy's trenches.

3. 1st Corps has placed a portion of the Heavy Artillery at the disposal of 2nd Division for the bombardment.
    The bombardment will take the form of destruction of part of the enemy's line opposite "A" Section and wire cutting in both "A" & "Z" Sections, Appendix A.

4. O.C., "A" Group will take charge of operations in "A" Section. The Heavy Artillery attached and 47th Howitzer Battery is placed at his disposal.

1st PHASE.

5. At 8 a.m. 15th December O.C., "A" Group will inform G.O.C., 5th Infantry Brigade whether the weather conditions permit of observation of fire. If at that hour the conditions are not favourable O.C., "A" Group will report again at 8-30 a.m., and if necessary every half hour up to 10-30 a.m. If at 10-30 a.m. the conditions still preclude observation the bombardment will be postponed.
    If observation is possible, G.O.C., 5th Infantry Brigade will clear certain trenches and will inform O.C., "A" Group as soon as the trenches are clear. The bombardment will them commence.
    O.C., "A" Group will inform G.O.C., 5th Infantry Brigade as soon as the heavy bombardment in the Brickstacks is completed. Fire will be maintained for a further period during the re-occupation of the trenches.

2nd. PHASE.

6. Divisional Headquarters will decide at 10-0 p.m. whether the operation is to proceed or not.
    (a) If orders are given for the operation to proceed the gas will be discharged at midnight. It is estimated that all the gas will be discharged in ten minutes.
    No fire will be opened until it is clear that the enemy has taken the alarm.
    (b) When the enemy takes the alarm and opens fire, the artillery will open fire on the German communication trenches, and maintain for half an hour. No fire will be opened unless the enemy takes the alarm and opens fire.
    (c) In the event of heavy rifle and machine gun fire being opened by the enemy, the artillery will shell the German front line in addition to the communication trenches.

    All fire to be directed East of the German support line after 12.25 a.m. so as not to endanger our raiding parties.

2.

(d) Unless the rifle and machine gun fire from the enemy's parapet at the end of the gas attack proves conclusively that the gas has had no effect on the enemy, raids will be made on the enemy's trenches (Appendix D) preceded by scouts at 12-25 am.

(e) An artillery officer will be detailed to the Headquarters of each Battalion finding a raiding party. ~~Artillery fire will only be opened at the instructions of the Battalion Commander to this officer.~~

(f) 18-pr. fire may also be opened at the request of the Battalion Commander to cover the retirement of the parties. In this case a barrage will be put on any of the following points :-

   A 28 a 8 9
   A 22 c 2 2   A 22 c 2 7
   A 22 a 2 7
   A 16 c 2 2
   A 16 c 3 3

7. It must be understood that the bombardment and the gas operation are independent of each other. Either or both, or neither, may be carried out according to the state of the weather.

          Major, R.A.,
      Brigade Major, R.A., 2nd Division.

Issued at 10.30 p. to :-

 Copy No. 1 A Group.
  ,, 2 Z Group.
  ,, 3 34th Brigade.
  ,, 4 44th Brigade.
  ,, 5 59th Siege Battery.
  ,, 6 Div. Amm. Column.
  ,, 7 & 8 2nd Division.
  ,, 9 H.A., 1st Corps)
  ,, 10.R.A., 12th Division) For information.
  ,, 11 R.A., 15th Division)

APPENDIX A.

1st PHASE.

UNIT	TIME	TARGET	AMMUNITION	REMARKS
"A" Group.				
Section 10th Siege Battery	0-0 to about* 3-0	Brickstacks A 21 b 8 8 to A 15 d 9 3	100	To demolish all works especially mine shafts.
3rd Siege Battery		Line A 32 a 4 7 to A 16 c 5 3	250	Fire at a slower rate after 3-0 hours. *according to progress.
47th Howitzer Battery	0-0 to 4-0	Support trenches North and South of Brickstacks.	300	Especially Minenwerfer positions.
56 Howitzer Battery				
3 18-pr. Batteries.	0-0 to 3-0	Wire 1. A 21 b 8 6 2. A 15 d 9 4	400	
	0-0 to 4-30	Approaches.	400	H.E.
"Z" Group.	as required.	Wire A 28 a 0 2 A 27 b 9 7 A 21 d 6 0 A 21 d 6 5	600	

2nd PHASE.

"A" Group	Night lines (Para.6 e)	as required	According to circumstances at infantry request.
"Z" Group.	Communication trenches (Para.6 b)		
18-pr. batteries	Barrage (Para. 6 f)		

APPENDIX B.

Scouts will start at 12-25 a.m. If the scouts are able to advance parties will follow.

PARTY	FOUND BY	FROM ABOUT	OBJECTIVE
A	6th Infantry Brigade.	R_1	Along railway to A 28 a 0 2.
B	- do -	T_1	A 27 b 9 7.
C	- do -	BOYAU 14	Along railway to MINE POINT A 21 d 6 0.
D	- do -	- " - 18	A 21 d 6.5
E	5th Infantry Brigade.	Just N. of LA BASSEE ROAD	A 21 b 8 6.
F	- do -	PALL MALL.	A 15 d 9 4.

2nd Divisional Artillery Orders

By Brigadier-General G.H.Sanders D.S.O., Commanding R.A.2nd Dn.

15th December 1915.

1184 R.A.ORDERS

Were not issued yesterday 14th December.

1185 LEAVE.

(a) Leave to officers during the Winter months will not be granted when the Division is in the RESERVE AREA, except under very exceptional circumstances, as it is most essential then that officers should be present with their units, for training purposes

(b) Cases are still occurring of men going on leave with ammunition in their possession, strict disciplinary action will be taken if this practice is not put a stop to at once.

1186 POSTINGS.

Captain E.W.Griffith, 2nd D.A.C. to command 44th B.A.C. vice Capt.Le SEUER posted to Home Estabt. with effect from 12th Decr. 1915.

Lieut.G.Messervy, 16th Battery, to do the duties of Capt. in 41st Bde.without temporary rank, vice Capt.D.C.Stephenson posted to Home Est. with effect from 14th Decr. 1915.

Lieut.F.L.V.Mills, 71st Battery, to do the duties of Capt. in 34th Bde. but without temporary rank, vice Capt.I.C.Pory Knox Gore 70th Battery, posted to Home Est. with effect from the 14th Dec.1915.

1187 A.F.B 231.

Attention is called to "INSTRUCTIONS FOR PREPARING A.F.B. 231 dated 2nd May 1915", Note to para 3 (b) which states :-
"It is assumed that 'other ranks' have been evacuated out of the Divl.Area 3 days after admission to hospital, unless their names are notified as being in the Divl.Coy."

1188 STEEL HELMETS.

The issue of helmets on the following scale was recommended to 1st Corps on 17-11;15 :-

4 per R.F.A.Bde.H.Q.(for use of observing offr.
10 per battery R.F.A.(and signallers
but the issue has not yet been approved, and indents submitted to D.A.D.O.S. cannot be met until such approval has been received.

sd L.G.BUXTON Captain R.A.

Staff Captain R.A. 2nd Dn.

DIARY   Ra 2 Div
DATE
15.12.15

OBSERVATION CONDITIONS. From No 7.15 – 4.10. Light fair.
Wind SSE Strong to SW later. Misty.

WORK DONE BY ENEMY.

nil

MOVEMENT SEEN.
    SW of ANTELEUX 9 am and 3/pm
    A10a5.2 10.30 – 11.30
    Near Lone Farm 7.45 – 8.30
    Lone Farm to A29a9½ 2½ – 12 men moving hard 8 am
    No organized body.

GUNS LOCATED OR SUSPECTED.

nil

WORKING PARTIES SEEN.
    A22d 3.3
    A29a 4.5

GENERAL. Lamp signalling again seen at Douvrin 7.45 – 8.10 am
SU 22 VERBAND CY-O HABEN ANGEBEN EBEN WIEVIEL
FEHLEN MELDEN AUSGENOMME. - - - - KK.
    message received & acknowledged with general answers.
GEIR NEIN   R III KOMEWILLY NACH IONURIN ADLFI
VETEEDL KOMME SEAE AR
    Bombardment of brickstack area carried out according to
programme. Numerous loopholes in D E F G & H brickstacks
revealed, and a large excavation in D apparently destroyed.
Wood revealed in many places in Stacks.
    Enemy make no great retaliation.
    Wire cut in several places – separate report.
ACTION.   See over.
                                        Lt. Colonel,
                                        Commanding

| ACTION Time | | Battery | Target | Rounds | Remarks |
From	To				
11.30	1.30	48	Wire	325	
11.45		17	Wire	307	
10	1	47	Programme	151	support trenches A1
10	2	56	---	200	--- A2
10.15	2	50	Wire	11	
		16	Wire		
1	2.30	50 ⎫ 16 ⎬ 71 ⎭	Dug outs in 2nd line & communications	50 50 50	

No other action of importance

ACTION Time From	To	Battery	Target	Rounds	Remarks
8·35	9·35	71	MOUND A17a5·5	16	Retaliation
9 A		56	Enemy seen S.W of CANTELEUX	13	
"		16	Movement seen A22 a 2·6	4	
10 AM	2 PM	49 / 56	ENEMY'S 2ND line by Brickstacks	200 / 200	
11·25		71	CANAL Trench	40	Retaliation
10·15	2 PM	50 / 16	Wire Cutting at A15d 9·5 and A21 c 7·5	210	
1	2·30	50 / 16 / 71	Enemy dug outs in 2ND line & Communications	50 / 50 / 60	

DIARY

DATE Dec 15th 1915.

OBSERVATION CONDITIONS. Observation possible 7.15 AM to 3.50 PM. Light good wind SSE strong.

WORK DONE BY ENEMY. Bombardment of Brickstacks to-day revealed numerous loopholes in D E F G & H Brickstacks and a large excavation was apparently destroyed on the top of D Brickstack. Wood was revealed in many places on the Brickstacks.

MOVEMENT SEEN. Enemy were seen in the open S.W. of CANTELEUX at 9 AM and 3 PM and were fired on by 56 Battery. A few of the enemy were also seen about A10a 52 at intervals between 10.30 and 11.30 AM. No organized bodies of enemy seen.

GUNS LOCATED OR SUSPECTED. "NIL".

WORKING PARTIES SEEN. "NIL".

GENERAL. 50th Batty (1 gun at A 8.c.5.1.) Wire cut at A.15.d.9.5 Range 1950 - There appears to be a clear gap of from 5 to 10 yards. It is difficult to say what damage has been done to the parapet. 200 Rounds fired.

16th Batty. (F 24.c.9.3) Wire cut at A.21.b.8.5 Range 2600 - No distinct gap has been made but the posts have been broken and the wire flattened down. I cannot say that any appreciable damage was done to the parapet, but I did not see it from a close range. 30 H Shrapnel. 20 H.E.

ACTION. See over.

H. Ward.
Lt. Colonel,
Commanding "A" Group

ACTION Time		Battery	Target	Rounds	Remarks
From	To				
8am		9th Batt	Germans in A22b 9.9	9	
9.48am		"	A30b 25.4	12	working
12.30pm			A16a 9.6	12	retaliation
2.10pm			German wire opp A1 South.	15	
8.35am		15th Batt	Lone farm	5	a few Germans
11am	1pm		Culvert A16c 4.8	26	
7.43am	8.10	17th Batt	Lone farm + vicinity	11	
10.20am			A29a 4.5	8	working party
11am			A22d 3.3	9	" "
11.45am			Cutting wire between rail'ys + POPES nose	307	see report
		17th Batt. own not retaliate being engaged in W.C.			
10am	1pm	47th	Bombardment	151	under orders A group
8. am		48th	PEKIN alley	6	Germans on top of tr.
8.15			Lone farm	9	Germans
3.50pm			Mad alley	4	" "
11.30a	1.30pm		Wire cutting in Rail'y to N of Popes nose	325	see report no retaliation by 48th
11am	11.30am	71st gun	Railway	20	retaliation
1pm	1.30pm	"	Les Bougnies	20	"
11.00am		59th Siege	A17d 8.9	12	BAP Hostile batteries

BR

DIARY.

DATE 15-12-15

OBSERVATION CONDITIONS. Observation possible 7.15 am till 4.10 pm mediocre to moderate.

WORK DONE BY ENEMY.

MOVEMENT SEEN. A few germans were seen near Lone farm also on top of Mad alley. 7.45 to 8.20 am. A party of twelve was seen at 8 am near Lone farm running very fast to A.29.a.95.25 were they fell into a trench

GUNS LOCATED OR SUSPECTED.

WORKING PARTIES SEEN. at A.22.d.3.3 and A.29.a.4.5

GENERAL. Lamps signalling again seen in Douvrin 7.43 am to 8.10 am message more intelligible today. see attached.
Report on W.C. today attached.

ACTION.   See over.

Roddell Lt
a.g.
for Lt. Colonel,
Commanding Z Group

2nd Divisional Artillery

HOSTILE   FIRE   REPORT.

15th December, 1915.

1. GENERAL INFORMATION.

The 4" gun which fired to-day does not seem very effective. It appears to be low velocity.

2 HOSTILE FIRE.

No.	Time From	to	Nature	Direction from	Area shelled	Remarks
1	7-30a		5.9 H.E.	VIOLAINES	GIVENCHY	20 Rounds.
2	9-30a		-			
3	10-30a	2-0p	77 mm. 4"Naval		A2 Sector CUINCHY	Intermittent 50% 4"were blind.
4	11-0a	12-50p	77 mm.		SPOIL BANK	25 Rounds.
5	11-30a		,,		CAMBRIN	
6	11-55a	12-5p	,,		A 20 d	Including 3 hits on WILSONS & GREENWOODS HOUSE. No damage.
7	12-45p		4" gun		A 19 d 7 3	1 air burst H.E.
8	12 noon		77 mm.	A U C H Y	Z1	A few.
9	3-15p		H.V.gun.		BEUVRY (?)	1 Round.

R Scott 2nd Lieut RA
for Major, R.A.,
Brigade Major, R.A., 2nd Divn.

1606

DAILY AMMUNITION RETURN

DATE 15 Dec: 15.

BATTERIES.

Piece	Projectile	Code	50	70	15	48	71	9	16	17	47	56	Total	Per Piece
18-pr	Guns.......													
	Shrapnel...	"A"	286	87	35	71	14	37	217	87	–	–	834	
	H. E.......	"Ax"	11	128	–	8	96	21	–	24	–	–	288	
4.5"	Howitzers..													
	Shrapnel...	"B"									–	–	–	
	H. E.......	"Bx"									53	216	269	

Wire cutting by 2nd Div. Artillery
15/12/15

Battery	Position	Target	Range	Rounds	Effect
How 48	A25b18	A27b96	2400	325	Two small gaps 40 yards apart and wire well damaged between. gap 5' wide
1½H. 17	F24a82	A28a02	2800	307	
7½H. 50(15m)	A8c51	A15d95	1950	200	Clear gap 5-10'
7½H. 16	F24c93	A21b85	2600	30 4.5h 20 H.E.	No distinct gap but posts all broken and wire much flattened.
					No appreciable damage to parapets in any case.

Later gap
10 yards

R.A. 2 Div
15.12.15

Mowbray
Major
BMRA

"A" Form.
Army Form C. 2121.
MESSAGES AND SIGNALS.

TO: Bde RA 12 Bde 186 Coy RE 2 Div Sig
BDE RE 17 Div 185 Coy RE
ADMS Troops 97 Cy RE

Sender's Number: GA 94
Day of Month: 15
AAA

Reference 2nd Div Operation Warning Order No 77 aaa Second phase of operations is postponed until further notice aaa Addressed addresses of 2 Div OO 77 and 47th Div.

Phone

Rec'd 10.5 pm

From: 2 Div
Time: 9.35 pm

R.a 7 Div. DIARY

DATE 16 Dec. 1915

OBSERVATION CONDITIONS. Light bad all day. Observation possible 7.30 to 3.40. Wind S. moderate.

WORK DONE BY ENEMY.

Wiring in Support Trench 20.
Repair to wire cut A 21 b 8 5

MOVEMENT SEEN.
Party carrying large white bundles (Sandbags?) moving towards
LA BASSEE A 22 a 5.0.
Party carrying planks behind LONE FARM.
Party of about 30 near CANTELEUX CROSS ROADS, 8.30 a.m.
Occasional Germans coming and going by CANTELEUX ALLEY S.,
which is probably waterlogged.

GUNS LOCATED OR SUSPECTED.

nil

WORKING PARTIES SEEN.

nil

GENERAL.
Enemy had agains's retaliation on usual targets between main road and canal, employing — 2 77mm. batteries of 4 guns
1 4.2" battery " " "
1.45 — 2.45 pm 1 5.9" battery " " "
average rate of fire 12 shells per minute. 1 4" Battery 2 time fuzes.
2.45 — 3.45"
6 shells per minute.
No serious damage done.
Further signalling from DOUVRIN — see attached —
Some trolleys were seen in trolley line behind
Sap in lines A 22 b 7 6

In continuation of wire cutting report — Sap at A 21 b 8 5
was 10ˣ clear — Sap at A 15 d 9 5 was 8ˣ clear. Not yet repaired —

ACTION. See over.

ACTION Time From	To	Battery	Target	Rounds	Remarks
8 a	8.45 a	71	CANTELEUX Crossroads Searching - Canteleux alley	50	Movement
9 p	9.45 p	71	Minnies A.17.a.6.7 A.16.a.2.2 A.15.a.8.9		
			M.G. Emplacement A.16.a.2.8	80	Retaliation
1.30	2.45	56	Embankment west R—	184	"
1.45	3.45	50	2nd Line strong points	750	"
1.35	3.30	16	Do. Tilbury St. A.22.a.5.7	72	"
9.40	10.45	9	A.22.b.7.8		Working party - several dropped
		9			
1.45	2.30	17	Haisnes & Auchy	63	Retaliation
1.30	2.30	48	Auchy & Mine Pt	60	Retaliation

ACTION

Time From	To	Battery	Target	Rounds	Remarks
8 AM	8.45	71	CANTELEUX cross roads searching N.E & CANTELEUX ALLEY SOUTH	50	Movement seen
9.30		56	A 10 d	4	Enemy seen
2 PM	2.45	71	Hounds A17a6.7 and A16a22 A15d8.9 & M.G Emplacement A16a 2.8	80	Retaliation
1.30	2.45	56	Enemys 2ND line EMBANKMENT FORT.	184	"
1.45	3.45	50	2ND line & strong points on our front	250	"
1.35	1.50	16	DISTILLERY & ROAD	32	"
3 PM	3.30	"	A 22 a 5.7	40	"

The Patrol from the 24th Battn. R. Fusiliers reported that a clear gap was cut in the wire which they walked straight through. This gap was about 10ft wide. The enemy have repaired it during the night. The gap made by the 50th Battn. is about 8 yards wide and has not been needed at all so far. The Tower of Bebel had two 9.2 trays into it, but I do not know what damage has been done at present but.

T. Ward Lt. Col.

DIARY

DATE DEC 16TH 1915.

OBSERVATION CONDITIONS. Light was bad all day observation possible 7.30 AM to 3.40 PM. Wind South Moderate

WORK DONE BY ENEMY. None observed.

MOVEMENT SEEN. 8 AM a party of about 30 GERMANS near CANTELEUX cross roads they were dispersed by 71 Battery.
8.30 AM to 10.30 occasional Germans seen going and coming CANTELEUX Alley South probably got out of the trench where it was waterlogged

GUNS LOCATED OR SUSPECTED. Nil

WORKING PARTIES SEEN. Nil

GENERAL. 1.45 to 3.40 PM Enemy had an organized retaliation on all the usual Targets between Main road and CANAL. Their Artillery employed appeared to be
2 77 mm Batteries 4 guns each.
1 4.2" Battery of 4 guns.
1 5.9" Battery " " "
1 4" gun Battery of three guns.
1.45 to 2.45 PM. average rate of fire 12 shells per minute including all qualities.
2.45 - 3.45 PM 6 rounds per minute including all qualities. No retaliation was observed from any of our Heavy Artillery. No serious damage was done
B Quiller Couch Lieut & Adj
for Lt. Colonel,
Commanding A group

ACTION. See over.

ACTION Time		Battery	Target	Rounds	Remarks
From	To				
9.40am		9t	A22b 7.8		working party
10.15am			A22b78 party leaving		MILL alley dispersed
			several were seen to fall		
10.30	10.45am		A22b78		party carrying timber
1.30pm	1.45pm		FRANKS keep	20	retaliation
7.55am		17th Batt	Lone farm	9	party carrying timber
1.45pm			Houses in Auchy	24	retaliation
2.30pm			Houses	39	"
3pm			party wiring in Support tr	6	
10.??	13/12/15	15th Bat	Madagascar tr	6	G request
8.15am	8.??		Mad point normals	3	
8.30am			Lone farm	4	Germans
1.55pm			Auchy	19	Retaliation
2.15pm			Madagascar tr	11	"
2.35pm			" "	17	"
11.45pm	15/12/15	59thS.	A28 a	4	retaliation
11.45pm	15/12/15	47th	Junc PEKIN & MAD ally	9	"
5pm	7pm	48?	Gap in wire	30	
7.15pm	9.50pm		" "	25	
10pm	4am		" "	41	
4.5am			Railway tr	4	G request
6.40am			" + support	16	"
1.30pm			Auchy	30	retaliation
2.30pm			Auchy + mine point	30	"

Z group DIARY.

DATE 16-12-15

OBSERVATION CONDITIONS.

BAD

WORK DONE BY ENEMY.

Worms in Support to Z0.

MOVEMENT SEEN. At 11.0 am a periscope was seen on N side of MINE pt. Shortly afterwards a german wearing a helmet got up and looked over quite leisurely.
A party carrying large white bundles (? of sandbags) seen moving towards La Bassee A22a 5.0.
Some planks were being carried behind Lone farm.

GUNS LOCATED OR SUSPECTED.

—

WORKING PARTIES SEEN.

—

GENERAL. A trolley line runs behind gap in houses A22 b 7.8
Some trolleys were observed.
The gun firing at 400' etc was coming at low velocity presumably from Haisnes.
More signals from Douvrin as per attached.

ACTION.   See over.

F. Roddh
Adj.
for Lt. Colonel,
Commanding

2nd Divisional Artillery

HOSTILE FIRE REPORT.

16th December, 1915.

1. GENERAL INFORMATION.

The gun which fired on O.Bs. seems to be a 4".
From 1-45p to 3-45p the enemy had an organised retaliation on the front between LA BASSEE Road and the CANAL.
77 mm,, 4.2" Hows. and 6" Hows. were employed in an obvious retaliation for our shoot yesterday. HOLLOW, CUINCHY, BULGE, PONT FIXE, KINGSCLERE and trenches and communication trenches were system~~ically~~ -atically fired on. The damage done was slight.

2. HOSTILE FIRE.

No.	Time From	To	Nature	Direction from	Area shelled	Remarks.
1.	1-40p	2-15p	100 mm. gun	HAISNES	BRADDELL Pt. in general	* 30 Rounds. Hits on "400" "RUIN" "TOWER OF BABEL"
2.	1-45p	3-40p	77mm 105mm 150mm 4" gun	HAISNES and S.LA BASSEE.	General Bombardment of A1 A2 B1	Shelling was heaviest on A2. Rate of fire about 12 shells per minute for 1st hour and 6 per minute the last.
3.	2-15p		77mm	?	Zo Trench	
4.	2-30p	2-50p	100mm	HAISNES	BRADDELL Pt in general	* 30 rounds.

* The same.

Major R.A.
Brigade Major R.A. 2nd Divn.

1611

DAILY AMMUNITION RETURN

DATE 16th Decr 1915

BATTERIES.

Piece	Projectile	Code	50	70	15	48	71	9	16	17	47	56	Total Per Piece
18-pr	Guns.......												
	Shrapnel...	"A"	203	134	19	469	29	52	111	313			1330
	H. E......	"Ax"	23	18	-	33	104	87	39	-			304
4.5"	Howitzers..												
	Shrapnel...	"B"									-	-	
	H. E......	"Bx"									144	87	201

2nd Div. RA DIARY.

DATE Dec 17· 1915

OBSERVATION CONDITIONS. Obs. possible as far as front trenches 8 am to 2.15 pm. Light bad all day. Some rain. Wind slight E.

WORK DONE BY ENEMY.

nil

MOVEMENT SEEN.

nil

GUNS LOCATED OR SUSPECTED.

nil

WORKING PARTIES SEEN.

nil

GENERAL.

Enemy have shown a little activity north of canal. South of canal only a few 77 mm shell fell by S.W. end of Tambières loop in A Section, but in Z section fired on various points - see Ine report.

ACTION.   See over.

                                   Lt. Colonel,
                                   Commanding

ACTION Time From	To	Battery	Target	Rounds	Remarks
16th					
8p	9p	71	Pekin alley	20	
10.30p	10.35p	48	Auchy	24	
10.30	11.45	71	Auchy - Mad alley	26	
11 p	4.30 a	48	Gap in wire	47	
7 a		71	A 16 a 9.6	2	Machine gun
9.15 a		56	Embankment R⁵	8	
10 a	10.15 a	17	Front tr. Z 2	17	work
10.25 a	10.35 a	17	"	18	"
10.55		56	Tortoise	7	
11.30 a	12.30 p	71	Auchy Harness Rd	24	
12 n.		48	La Bassée Rd	12	
12.19 p		47	A 21 d 7.1 Ryan keep	6	Retaliation to minnie
12.20	12.40	17	Snipers post	18	
1 p	2.30 p	71	A 17 a 5.5 A 16 a 11	30	Retaliation
1.15 p		15	Madagascar Tr.	22	Retaliation
2 p	3.30 p		Pope nose Hindenberg Dork alley Mad alley Auchy	60	"
2.5		17	Z 2 front	15	"
2.15		50	NE Brickstack	9	Corking pie
2.15	2.30	15	Madagascar Tr.	69	Bouquet
2.30	3	15	" "	27	"
			Lone Farm	67	"
2.45	3.10	16	A 22 a 2 8	30	Retaliation
3 p	3.50 p	15	Madagascar Tr.	10	"
3.15 p		71	Lone Farm	11	"
			Canteleux	18	"
3.50	4.5	15	Madagascar Tr.	53	"

2nd Divisional Artillery

HOSTILE FIRE REPORT.

17th December, 1915.

HOSTILE FIRE.

No.	Time From	To	Nature	Direction from	Area shelled	Remarks
1	10-15a	10-25a	77 mm.	A U C H Y	tr. A 27 b	9 Rounds.
2	11-45a	11-55a	,,	,,	A 26 b	8 ,,
3	12-45p	1-0p	,,	,,	A 27 d & b	25 ,,
4	1-0p	1-10p	,,	-	GIVENCHY	10 ,,
5	1-35p	2-50p	,,	A U C H Y	A 27 a & b	140 ,,
6	2-0p	3-50p	,, 4.2" H.E.	-	GIVENCHY	80 ,,
7	2-30p	2-38p	105 mm.	?	CAMBRIN E.	8 ,,
8	2-45p	2-55p	77 mm.	S. AUCHY	A 19 b 1 2	8 ,,
9	2-45p		,,	TRIANGLE	HEDGEROW Lane to LA BASSEE Rd.	10 ,,

Major, R.A.,
Brigade Major, R.A., 2nd Divn.

DAILY AMMUNITION RETURN

DATE 17.12.15

BATTERIES.

Piece	Projectile	Code	50	70	15	48	71	9	16	17	47	56	Total Per Piece
18-pr	Guns......												
	Shrapnel...	"A"	161	136	12	36	16	27	57	19	-	-	464
	H.E.......	"Ax"	116	180	93	92	90	20	1	97	-	-	689
4.5"	Howitzers..												
	Shrapnel...	"B"									-	-	-
	H.E.......	"Bx"									-	197	197

2nd Divisional Artillery Orders

by

Brigadier-General G.H.SANDERS, D.S.O., Comdg.R.A., 2nd Divn.

17th December,1915.

1189. COURTMARTIAL.

A F.G.C.M. will assemble at Headquarters, R.A., 2nd Division,(18 RUE SADI-CARNOT, BETHUNE) at 10 a.m. on Monday, 20th Decr.,1915, for the trial of No.75349 Dr. W.Jones, 36th Brigade, R.F.A., Ammn.Column, and such other accused as may be brought before it :-

PRESIDENT.
Major T.N.French.   -   47th Battery, R.F.A.

MEMBERS.
Captain R.Fernie.   -   41st B.A.C.
Lieutenant S.A.Kellagher. - 48th Battery, R.F.A.

The accused to be warned and all witnesses duly required to attend.

Proceedings to be forwarded to Staff Captain, R.A., 2nd Division.

Court Orderly to be supplied by 36th B.A.C.

L.G.BUXTON,Capt,R.A.
Staff Captain, R.A., 2nd Div.

DIARY. 2nd Div RA

DATE 18.12.15

OBSERVATION CONDITIONS. Obs possible 12.30 pm - 3 pm.; Bad them. Fog. Wind ESE light.

WORK DONE BY ENEMY. Pope pit large draining Embankment redoubt harbour laid. Many new Sandbags Embankment - A16c1.8. Infantry report much wood carried and repairs to trenches NE brickstack southward.

MOVEMENT SEEN.

nil

GUNS LOCATED OR SUSPECTED. A30 b 2.7 Pom fuzes picked up at A19 d 2 4 set at 5250 and scrape of shell

WORKING PARTIES SEEN.

nil

GENERAL.
Enemy fired at Cambrin at 12 noon and 3.30 pm

ACTION.   See over.   Lt. Colonel,
                                         Commanding

ACTION Time From	To	Battery	Target	Rounds	Remarks
17th					
8.45p	8.50p	47	Ryan Keep	6	Retaliation to Minnie
8.45	9 pm	9	Z 2 point	10	" "
10 h		48	Auchy	6	"
18th 12.15a		48	"	12	"
1.10 a		48	Mine point	4	"
1.20	2.10	15	Madagascar Tr.	200	" (by request)
8 a	10 a	71	Canteleux	40	Retaliation.
8.45	9.17	47	A 21 d trenches	8	Retaliation to Minnie.
9.28	9.30	47	Ryan Keep	4	
10		9	Z 2	5	
10.15		9	Auchy	25	
11.15	11.24	47	Ryan Keep	12	" "
11.30		50	Brickstacks + trenches	12	work. This started much retaliation.
12.10p		17	Haisnes	15	Retaliation.
12.20p		16	A 18 b 8.8	6	"
12.20p		9	Auchy	20	"
1 p	1.30	71	A 17 a 55	25	"
1.50p	1.56	47	Ryan Keep	16	"
3.25p		48	Mine Pt, Mad alley	15	"
3.30p	3.40	16	A 22 a trenches	10	"
			Battery A 30 b 7.6	10	"
3.30 p		48	Auchy	12	"
3.30 p		9	Z 2 point	14	"
3.35 p		17	Haisnes	12	"
4 p		59 Aug	Haisnes	1	
4.21 p		47	Ryan Keep	8	Retaliation to Minnie.
4.30 p	5	48	Haisnes La Bassée Rd.	17	

2nd Divisional Artillery
HOSTILE FIRE REPORT.

18th December, 1915.

1. General Information.

Much work with new sandbags has been done on EMBANKMENT redoubt and Trench A 16 c 1.8.

2. HOSTILE FIRE.

No.	Time From	To	Nature	Direction from.	Area Shelled.	Remarks.
1.	8-0a	10-0a	5.9") 4.2") 77mm)	VIOLAINES	GIVENCHY	One 5.9" firing 1 round every two mins. 3, 4.2" firing every min.
2.	11-30a	12 noon	77mm	HAISNES Cy.	CAMBRIN	12 rounds.
3.	12-5p	12-20p	77mm	AUCHY	BRADDELL Pt LA BASSEE Rd	26 rounds. 12 ,, 3 salvoes opp Bde.H.Q.
4.	12-40p		77mm	AUCHY	ditto	8 rounds. Probably same battery firing more East.
5.	1-0p	1-30p	5.9" 4.2"	VIOLAINES	GIVENCHY	
6.	3-30p		77mm	HAISNES	CAMBRIN	12 rounds.
7.	3-30p		77mm	AUCHY	See 3 & 4	20 rounds.
8.	9-10a) 1-40p) 3-22a)		Minenwerfer	MINE Point.		

Major R.A.
Brigade Major R.A. 2nd Divn.

DAILY AMMUNITION RETURN

DATE 18 Dec 1915

BATTERIES.

Piece	Projectile	Code	50	70	15	48	71	9	16	17	47	56	Total	Per Piece
18-pr	Guns.......													
	Shrapnel...	"A"	14	104	209	106	17	83	15	7	–	–	555	
	H. E......	"Ax"	–	175	–	17	67	15	9	27	–	–	310	
4.5"	Howitzers..													
	Shrapnel...	"B"									–	–	–	
	H. E......	"Bx"									36	3	39	

2nd Divisional Artillery Orders

By

Brig-General G. H. SANDERS, D.S.O., C. R. A. 2nd Division.

18th December 1915.

1190 COURTMATRIAL.

Major R ff Powell, 71st Battery R.F.A. will be President of the F.G.C.M. ordered to assemble on Monday 20th instant, vice Major T.N.French.

1191. SHOWER BATHS.

The new shower baths in BEUVRY near the billets of the Tunnelling Company are now open (No.58 on billet map). Units requiring them should apply Right Brigade in the line.

1192 RAILHEAD.

Until further orders BETHUNE will be railhead. All hours of reloading will be the same as at present.

1193. EMPTY CARTRIDGE CASES.

Empty 18-pr cartridge cases are still being returned to D.A.C. unpacked in boxes. As 8 empty cases can be packed in a box holding 4 complete rounds, there is an allowance of 50% loss in boxes; there is, therefore, no reason why all cases should not be packed in boxes. All spare boxes should now be sent to D.A.C.,until they have sufficient in hand to pack all cases found by Salvage Company, etc.

1194 DIVINE SERVICE.

C. E. 11 a.m. in the Divisional Concert Hall. Rue d'AIRE.
R. C. 8-30 a.m. in BETHUNE Cathedral.
Wes. 9-30 a.m. in the Divl.Recreation Room Rue des TREILLES.

1195. CORRESPONDENCE.

When for tactical reasons it is necessary to form special groups, and to adopt local titles, these titles should not be used in ordinary routine correspondence which has to be forwarded to offices outside the Corps, nor should they be used on Ordnance indents.

L. G. BUXTON Captain R.A.

Staff Captain R.A.2nd Dn.

DIARY. Ra 2nd Div

DATE Dec. 19. 1915

OBSERVATION CONDITIONS. Light very good all day. Obs possible 7.15 - ft. Wind NE moderate.

WORK DONE BY ENEMY. Gap at A15d9.5 has been mended - not so strong as before. Some sandbag work near culvert. Some wiring of a trench in A22a N. of Les Briques. Trench A22d5.0 SW toward railway - some work done. There is a work inside Les Briques trees with corr and air space above and loophole plates below.

MOVEMENT SEEN.
30 Germans on road Biqa going toward Douvrin 10.20 am
Some movement by Lone Farm
Small parties moving both ways between Canteleux & Violaines 7.30 am
Two or three men leaving trench A16c3.4 reluctantly and crawling in open (trench no doubt in bad repair)

GUNS LOCATED OR SUSPECTED.
11.50 am flashes judged at A17d9.1
Fire at A18a1.1 caused battery already reported to cease -
This spot is generally effective.
7.5 am flashes on line Fire Hundred - Mettalurgique water tower, behind Haisnes Ridge.

WORKING PARTIES SEEN.
7.30 am   by Lone Farm
10.8   A16a7.7
12.15   behind ham in Triangle
3.15   Tortoise front line
3.30   A16a3.3

GENERAL.
Enemy directed heavy howitzer fire on Givenchy intermittently all day - there were 5.9, 4.2 and possibly 6 in.
Lamp signals again seen from Douvrin 2.35 pm
There is a plank on top of the NE chimney of Wingles
Flash (possibly of telescope) noticed in Wingles water tower.

ACTION.   See over.   Lt. Colonel,
                                            Commanding

ACTION Time From	To	Battery	Target	Rounds	Remarks
5	5.5	47	Ryans Keep	16	
7	9	71	Auchy La Bassee Rd	10	
			Auchy Harnes Rd	10	
7.30	9	9	Lone Farm	15	Work
7.30	8.30	50 } 71 }	Canteleux Violaine Rd	22	Movement
7.45	8.50	48	various	32	Movement
		15	Les Briques	8	"
11.50		56	A 18 a 1.1	27	Bakery Silenced
12.15	1.45	56	Triangle	19	Work interrupted
12.30		9	Auchy A23c26	35	Suspected OP
1.30	2.40	48, 15 } 9, 47 }	Les Briques	134	new work. Some hits but more treatment needed
2.23		56	Culvert. new earth work	7	
2.30		71	A 10 d 1 4	20	new earthwork
3.15	3.30	56	{ Tortoise { A16 a 3.3	10	work in progress
4.10		15	Lone Farm	8	Movement

Other fire in retaliation

ACTION Time From	To	Battery	Target	Rounds	Remarks
5 pm	5.57 pm	47	Ryansheep	16	minnie
7 pm	9 pm	71	Auchy La Bassee Rd / Auchy Haisnes Rd	10 / 10	
9.30 pm		9	E of Gibsons Cro.	6	to stop minnie
10.30 pm	11 pm	9	second line	8	noise of mining
11 pm		17	Trenches	6	" "
12 mid	12.10 am	48	Auchy .. minen pk	32	retaliation
11.45 pm		9	Trenches	6	by request
7.30 am		9	N.E. Lone farm	15	Washing party
1 am	7.30 am	48	gaps in wire	30	
7.45 am	8.50 am	48	Various	32	germans
7.50 am		15	Les Briques. Lone fm	8	germans
12.10 am	12.20 am	17	Trenches	18	retaliation
12.30 pm		9	House in Auchy	35	suspected O.P. A23c.26
12.30 pm	12.40 pm	48	Dooh alley. minieph	10	retaliation
12.40	1.15 pm	17	Trenches	26	germans firing at an aeroplane
1.30 pm	2 pm	48	Emplacements in Les Briques	40	some hits but no result treatment to be repeated
2 pm		15	" "	12	"Weekly strong pt."
2.15 pm		9	" "	20	" " "
2.20 pm	3.15 pm	47	" "	34	" " "
2.40 pm		15	" "	28	" " "
2.45 pm	3 pm	71	Fosse support madagascar t	10	
4.10 pm		15	Lone farm	8	germans
4.55 pm		17	Trenches	12	
				593	S. did not shoot.

DIARY.

DATE

OBSERVATION CONDITIONS. Possible at 7.20 a.m. and good all day till 4.15 pm.

WORK DONE BY ENEMY. A trench in front of a cart N. of Les Brigues in A22a has been wired. Some work has been done on a tr running from A22d 5.0 SW towards railway.
A work inside Les Brigues trees has been noticed A22d 2.2 with cover and airspace above and loophole plates below. Probably a strong MG emplacement.

MOVEMENT SEEN. 30 germans seen near Rd B19a going towards DOUVRIN 10.20 am. Some movement seen round Low Farm during early morning.
Smoke of a train behind DOUVRIN going south.

GUNS LOCATED OR SUSPECTED.
At 7.5am flashes were seen on line FOURNES to Metallurgique Water tower apparently behind HAISNES ridge.

WORKING PARTIES SEEN. A party at 7.30am near Low farm to NE.

GENERAL. Lamp signals from DOUVRIN herewith at 2.35pm.
— German aeroplanes very active all day. At 4 pm a German monoplane very much resembling a Morane circled over CAMBRIN. It was apparently mistaken for a Morane until engaged by one of our Moranes. The difference being that it had no 'nick' or out of wings near body. ?FOKKER type.
— There is a plank on top of the N.E. of Wingles chimneys. The flash of what may have been a telescope was visible in the Wingles Water tower. (Metallurgique works.

ACTION. See over.

T. Roddah
Adj for
Lt.Colonel,
Commanding 2 Group.

ACTION

Time From	To	Battery	Target	Rounds	Remarks
9.30AM		71	TORTOISE	20	At request from Infantry
"		16	2ND line Trench	4	MINENWERFER.
11.45P		56	Behind A & D Brickstacks	12	"
7.30AM	8.30	50	ENEMY in open on CANTELEUX VIOLAINES ROAD	12	
		71		10	
10.45		16	LA BASSEE ROAD	12	Retaliation
11.50		56	A 18 a 1.1	27	Battery which stopped firing when engaged.
11.30	12	71	TORTOISE	60	Retaliation.
12.15	1.45	56	Enemy working behind TRAIN	19	Work interrupted.
2.23		56	New work near CULVERT	7	
2.?		71	New earthwork. A.18.d 1.4 & A.17.c.7.9	20	
2.30		50	EMBANKMENT REDOUBT	20	
3	4	16	A 22 d 7.3	20	Retaliation
3.15	3.30	56	Working party in TORTOISE & A16a 3.3	10	

DIARY

DATE 19/12/15

OBSERVATION CONDITIONS. Light very good all day. Observation possible 7.15 A.M. to 4 P.M. Wind N.E. Moderate.

WORK DONE BY ENEMY. The gap cut in the wire A 15 d 9.5 has now been mended. But it is not so strong as before at present. Some sand bag work has been done near the CULVERT.

MOVEMENT SEEN. Enemy were seen in small parties moving both ways between CANTELEUX and VIOLAINES at 7.30 A.M. Two or three men were seen to leave trench A 16 c 3.4 rather reluctantly and crawl along in the open. The trench here would therefore appear to be in bad repair.

GUNS LOCATED OR SUSPECTED.
At 11.50 A.M. Flashes were observed from HUN VIEW and placed on map at A 17 d 9.1. Fire at Battery previously reported about A 18 a 1.1 immediately caused them to stop firing. It nearly always stops firing when engaged at this point so is not properly located.

WORKING PARTIES SEEN.
10.8 A.M A 16 a 7.7
12.15 P.M Working behind tram on TRIANGLE
3.15 P.M Working in TORTOISE front line
3.30 P.M. A 16 a 3.3.

GENERAL.

The enemy fired their Heavy Howitzers at GIVENCHY intermittently all day about 160 rounds altogether. These appeared to come from WOODS S.E. of LA BASSEE.
5.9" and 4.2" Hows were certainly firing and 8" How is also reported. Our Heavy Artillery were not seen to retaliate on any of the enemy's front system of trenches.

B Quiller Couch.
Lieut & Adjt
for Lt.Colonel,
Commanding A Group

ACTION. See over.

2nd Divisional Artillery

HOSTILE FIRE REPORT.

19th December, 1915.

1. GENERAL INFORMATION.

Small parties of the enemy were seen walking between VIOLAINES and CANTELEUX and were fired on.

GIVENCHY was fired on with heavy shell intermittently throughout the day. Enemy leave their trench A 16 c 3 4 and crawl along the open. It is therefore presumed that it is in bad repair.

Enemy have been working on S.W. face of TRIANGLE.
11-50 a.m. flashes were seen A 17 d 9 1 from HUN VIEW.

2. HOSTILE FIRE.

No.	Time From	Time To	Nature	Direction from	Area shelled	Remarks.
1.	8-10a	8-20a	77 mm.	A U C H Y	Tr.A 27 c	
2.	8-45a	10-15a	5.9" or 8"	COISNE CHATEAU	GIVENCHY	About 60 Rounds.
3.	10-10a	10-40a	77 mm.	A U C H Y	MAISON ROUGE Ridge.	30 Rounds, 3 hits on 'Babe'- no damage.
4.	10-45a		77 mm.	?	CAMBRIN	10 Rounds.
x 5.	12-20p		,,	?	,,	20 ,,
6.	12-30p	2-45p	8" 5.9" 4.2"	East of LA BASSEE	GIVENCHY	100 ,,
7.	1-30p	2-30p	4"gun	?	ANNEQUIN	40 ,,
8.	3-0p		77 mm.	?	A 21 b 5 4	

x (?) a.m.

Major, R.A.,
Brigade Major, R.A., 2nd Divn.

DAILY MUNITION RETURN.

Piece	Projectile	Code	50	70	15	48	71	9	16	27	47	53			Total	Per piece
2.75	Guns															
	Shrapnel	P														
	H.E.	PX														
18-pr	Guns															
	Shrapnel	A		19	105	37	102	23	52	18	18				374	385
	H.E.	AX		—	84	101	36	43	22	36	63					
4.5" How.	Howitzers															
	Shrapnel	B									—	—				107
	H.E.	BX									40	67				
6" How	Howitzers															
	Shrapnel	H														
	H.E.	F														
	A.P.															

1622

2nd Divisional Artillery Orders

by

Brigadier-General G.H.SANDERS, D.S.O.,Comdg.R.A., 2nd Divn.

19th December,1915.

1196. SHELL.- PIECES OF PREMATURE

Any portions of Shell, which are found after an H.E. premature, should be returned to railhead for transmission to the Director General of Munitions Design, in exactly the same condition as found.

L.G.BUXTON, Capt, R.A.

Staff Captain, R.A., 2nd Division.

DIARY. RA 2nd Div

16244

DATE 20.12.15

OBSERVATION CONDITIONS. Obs possible 8am - 3pm.
Light very bad all day. Wind N. backing to N.W.

WORK DONE BY ENEMY.

nil

MOVEMENT SEEN.

nil

GUNS LOCATED OR SUSPECTED.

nil

WORKING PARTIES SEEN.

1.20 am A16 a 2 3 (Infantry report)

GENERAL.

No artillery activity by enemy. We fired
a good deal in retaliation to Minnies.

ACTION.   See over.   Lt.Colonel,
                                  Commanding

ACTION					
Time		Battery	Target	Rounds	Remarks.
From	To				
9h		71	Cantileux La Bassée Rd. obs: fire in retaliation	30	Transport — it retired rapidly.

ACTION Time From	To	Battery	Target	Rounds	Remarks
9 pm	7 am	9	night lines	22	by request at various times
9.20 am		9	second line	30	retaliation
9.35 am		17	Trenches	12	"
9.36	9.45	47	Ryans keep	7	" to minnie
9.45		9	Trenches	15	" "
9.55	10.1	47	Ryans keep. A21a 7.1	16	" "
10 am		17	Trenches	12	"
10 am		15	Madagascar t.	22	"
10.17 am		17	Working party	7	
12.46 pm		17	Snipers post	18	by request (near ETNA)
1. pm		47	Ryans keep. A21a 21	16	retaliation to minnie
1.55 pm		47	" "	32	" "
2.5 pm		48	tr behind Lone farm	6	"
2.5 pm		17	Trenches	9	"
2.10 pm		48	Popes nose	18	"
2.15 pm		9	Trenches	10	"
2.20 pm		17	"	9	"
2.40 pm		71 gun	Forme support	4	
2.45 pm		17	Trenches	8	"
3 pm		9	Auchy	20	"
3.45 pm		48	minnie point	2	checking lines

DIARY. Z group

DATE 20/12/15

OBSERVATION CONDITIONS. Very bad all day, possible at 8.55 am.

WORK DONE BY ENEMY.

MOVEMENT SEEN.

Nothing to report today.

GUNS LOCATED OR SUSPECTED.

WORKING PARTIES SEEN.

GENERAL.

ACTION.   See over.

Roald L
Adj.
for Lt.Colonel,
Commanding Z group.

ACTION Time		Battery	Target	Rounds	Remarks
From	To				
9 PM		71	CANTELEUX LA BASSEE Rd	30	Transport heard which retired rapidly
1.20 AM		71	A 16 a 2.3	12	Working party which was interrupted.
9.20 A		16 56	MINNIE in 2nd line just N of LA BASSEE Road.	16 5	
10.30		50	NE Brickstack	10	Trench mortars active
11 AM	12 noon	71	New Earthworks A 17 c 6-8½	45	Firing on this target produced retaliation
2.45 PM		16	MAIN LA BASSEE road - A 22 b	10	Retaliation for 3 rounds fired at Barrier.
"		71	2ND line in TORTOISE	10	Retaliation

DIARY

DATE 20/12/15

OBSERVATION CONDITIONS. Observation possible 8 AM till 3 PM. Light very bad all day wind N in morning backing to N W about 1 PM.
Observation seldom possible beyond front line.

WORK DONE BY ENEMY. None seen.

MOVEMENT SEEN. None seen.

GUNS LOCATED OR SUSPECTED. NIL.

WORKING PARTIES SEEN. 1.20 A M A 16 a 2 3 reported by Infantry

GENERAL. Enemy have been fairly active with small Trench mortars from their Brickstacks otherwise 24 Hours has been extremely quiet

ACTION. See over.

B Quiller Couch
Lieut & Adjt
for Lt.Colonel,
Commanding A Group

2nd Divisional Artillery

HOSTILE FIRE REPORT.

20th December, 1915.

1. GENERAL INFORMATION.

Observation impossible.

2. HOSTILE FIRE.

No.	Time From	To	Nature	Direction from	Area shelled	Remarks
1.	9-40a	9-50a	77 mm.	?	Z1 Z0 trenches	30 Rounds.
2.	12-5 p	12-30p	,,	LA BASSEE	GIVENCHY	20 ,,
3.	1-30p	1-45p	,,	,,	,,	10 ,,
4.	2-0 p	2-15p	,,	?	Opp. MINE Pt. RUSSELLS KEEP	12 ,,
5.	2-15p	3-0 p	,, 105 mm.	?	Opposite MINE POINT.	25 ,,
6.	2-45p		77 mm.	N. of road.	CAMBRIN EAST.	6 ,,
7.	2-45p		,,	LA BASSEE	BARRIER	4 ,,

Major, R.A.,
Brigade Major, R.A. 2nd Divn,

1626

DAILY AMMUNITION RETURN

DATE 20th Decr. 1915

BATTERIES.

Piece	Projectile	Code	50	70	15	48	71	9	16	17	47	56	Total	Per Piece
18-pr	Guns......													
	Shrapnel...	"A"	25	62	50	67	46	42	23	68			383	
	H.E......	"Ax"	31	34	26	51	75	142	9	14			382	
4.5"	Howitzers..													
	Shrapnel...	"B"												
	H.E......	"Bx"									57	69	126	

2nd Divisional Artillery Orders

by

Brigadier-General G.H.SANDERS, D.S.O.,Comdg.R.A., 2nd Division.

20th December,1915.

1197. PROMOTION.

Os.C.Brigades and D.A.C.,should submit names of Temporary Officers recommended for promotion by the evening of 23rd December,1915.

L.G.BUXTON, Capt, R.A.,
Staff Captain, R.A., 2nd Divn.

DIARY

DATE 21-XII-15.

OBSERVATION CONDITIONS. Rather misty all day - Observation possible from 10am to 3-30 pm - Only the enemy's front line could be seen.

WORK DONE BY ENEMY. — none observed —

MOVEMENT SEEN. — nil —

GUNS LOCATED OR SUSPECTED. Machine gun located in EMBANKMENT; 20 yards N.W. of culvert which was active at 10-15 pm on the 20th.

WORKING PARTIES SEEN. — none —

GENERAL. At 10-15 pm, 20-XII-15, the enemy opened machine gun fire, at 10-16 pm he lit a fire on EMBANKMENT REDOUBT, then two more and then 10 more at intervals of 90 yards along CANAL TRENCH and TORTOISE. From 10-25 to 11-15, 4·2" How fired on our trenches N of Canal, and at 10-40, following two red lights, 77mm battery fired on A2. Shelling at 11-5 pm. Everything normal at 11-45. A small searchlight was seen N of Canal possibly in 3rd line trench. The fire to have caused by M Gun being turned on in the Northern Sector.

ACTION.   See over.

B.B.Myndoch
ffor Lt.Colonel,
Commanding A group

Action Time From	To	Battery	Target	Rounds	Remarks
20 – XII – 15					
8-35 pm		16	Enfilade LA BASSÉE ROAD	8	Retaliation
8-45 pm		71	CANAL TRENCH	25	at request of Infantry
10-20 pm		50	TRENCHES	45	Retaliation, – do –
11-20 pm		56	TRENCHES N of Canal	15	– do – to 4.2" shelling
21 – XII – 15					
6-30 am		71	CANAL TRENCH	10	– do –
10-15 am		71	CANTELEUX	25	– do –
10-30 am		56	CANAL HOUSE	17	– do – 77mm on CUINCHY
11-10 am		16	TRENCHES A22a	18	– do –
11-20 am, 11-40 am, 12-5 p, 1-25 p, 2-37, 2-51, 3-10		50	Enemy trenches N of Canal and Embankment Redoubt and N.E. Brickstack	70	R do – destroyed a loophole at A.16.a.1-1 Several direct hits
11-55 am		16	TRENCHES A22a	6	Retaliation
11-55		56	on MINENWERFEN	21	at request of H.L.I.
12-10		71	FRONT TRENCHES	20	registration
12-15		16	Support trenches	22	Retaliation to MINENWERFER
1-15		71	Support trenches	25	– do –
2-0		56	CULVERT	22	– do – our trenches being shelled with 4" naval gun
2-30 p		71	Work S of CANTELEUX	20	
2-45 p		56	CULVERT	7	Retaliation to shelling of PONT FIXE.
2-45		16	TRENCHES A22-48	12	– do –
3-0		56	TRAIN	16	5.9" shelling PONT FIXE.
3-15		56	TRENCH MORTAR S of LA BASSÉE RD	7	

DAILY DIARY Z Group.

DATE 21.12.15.

OBSERVATION CONDITIONS. Possible at 7.45am, rest of the day very bad.

WORK DONE BY ENEMY.

Nothing to report.

MOVEMENT SEEN. Some working parties were seen near LONE FARM. and dispersed.
At 1pm Brushwood was seen being carried into FRANKS KEEP.

GUNS LOCATED OR SUSPECTED.
A 4 gun battery was located in A23 a 5.6, and its flashes observed at 10.40pm last night

WORKING PARTIES SEEN.
As above.

GENERAL.
At 10.30 pm enemy opened fire with rifles and machine guns, just south of Canal.
Fires were lit in trenches near RAILWAY TRIANGLE.
At 3pm Trench mortar active on LA BASSEE ROAD.

ACTION. See over. Lieutenant,
Commanding

ACTION Time		Battery	Target	Rounds	Remarks
From	To				
10.40 pm		9th Bty.	Bty A.23.a.6.5.		
10.30 am		do	German Communication Trenches 1st and 2nd Line		Retaliation.
3 pm		do	Trenches near LA BASSEE ROAD		Searching for Minenwerfer just South of Road.
1.30 pm		15 Bty	LONE FARM.	13	Checking registration from new platform.
2.45 pm		do	Trenches.	15	Retaliation by request of infantry.
7.55 am		17th Bty	Working Party	8.	Dispersed.
9.25 am		do	few men in the open	3.	
10.35 am	11.5 am	do	German 1st Line	70.	Retaliation.
12.54 pm		do	Work A.29.a.2.1	17.	Party seen here & dispersed.
12.58 pm		47th Bty	RYANS KEEP and A.21.d.7.1.	8.	In retaliation to Minenwerfer.
2.15 pm		do	AUCHY.	12	do to 4.2" H.
10.30 am	11. am	48 Bty	Enemy 1st & 2nd Line	20	In retaliation.
11 am	12 noon	do	LA BASSEE ROAD	24.	
1.30 pm	2. pm	do	Enemy 1st & 2nd Line	33	In retaliation to enemy shelling Z.1
2.15 pm	2.30 pm	do	do	18	
3. pm	3.15 pm	do	Enemy front line	8	do
		59th Bty RGA.	Did not fire to-day.		

R.W. Reeves. 2/L
for adj 41st Bde
RFA.

2nd Divisional Artillery

HOSTILE FIRE REPORT.

21st December, 1915.

1. GENERAL INFORMATION.

Hostile guns located in A 23 a 5 6. Flashes of same at 10-40p.m. (20th).
Observation possible - 10 a.m. to 2-30 p.m.

2. HOSTILE FIRE.

No.	Time From	To	Nature	Direction from	Area shelled	Remarks.
	20th.					
1.	8-30p		77 mm.	A U C H Y	HARLEY ST.	10 Rounds.
2.	10-15p	10-35p	4.2"	VIOLAINES	HOLLOW and Embankment	10 ,,
3.	10-25p	10-40p	4.2"	A U C H Y	CUINCHY Support Point	20 ,,
4.	10-40p		Light Field gun.	,,	A1 Trenches	4 gun battery
	21st.					
5.	7-20a	11-30a	4.2"	VIOLAINES	Road from PONT FIXE to WINDY CORNER	10 Rounds.
6.	10-30a		Heavy guns	A U C H Y	Z 2 Trenches	
7.	10-30a	11-15a	77 mm.	Unknown	A 21 d	60 rounds in salvos of 3.
8.	11-5a		77 mm.	A U C H Y	Z2 Trenches	8 Rds. in salvos of 4.
9.	12-5p	12-15p	,,	LA BASSEE	HOLLOW ~~x. of xxxxx.~~	15 Rds. ~~20 ,, of which 15 blind.~~
10.	12-55p	1-0p	10 cm.	Unknown	A 21 d	12 Rds.
11.	1-5p		77 mm.	,,	A 27 b	10 ,,
12.	1-35p	1-50p	10cm.	,,	Trenches N. of CANAL.	20 Rds. of which 15 blind.
13.	2-10p	2-20p	4.2"	,,	A 27 b	21 Rds. 30% blinds.
14.	2-35p	3-5p	5.9") 77 mm.)	SALOME (?)* Unknown	PONT FIXE	10 Rds 10 ,,

* Perhaps DOUVRIN.

R. Scott
2/Lieut R.A Major, R.A.,
Brigade Major, R.A.2/Divn.

DAILY AMMUNITION RETURN

DATE 21st Decr. 1915.

BATTERIES.

Piece	Projectile	Code	50	70	15	48	71	9	16	17	47	56	Total	Per Piece
18-pr	Guns.......													
	Shrapnel...	"A"	61			59	32	45	33	18			248	
	H. E.......	"Ax"	15			4	83	46	14	92			254	
4.5"	Howitzers..													
	Shrapnel...	"B"												
	H. E.......	"Bx"									48	32	80	

1631

DIARY.

DATE 22-12-15

OBSERVATION CONDITIONS. Possible at 7.30 am but poor all day. Failed at 3.45 pm

WORK DONE BY ENEMY.

MOVEMENT SEEN. Enemy left their trenches in A22 d 5.4 and proceeded towards AUCHY

GUNS LOCATED OR SUSPECTED. Flashes bearing 90° & 100° mag from A 20 d 5.6½ 8.5 pm 21-12-15

WORKING PARTIES SEEN.

GENERAL.

Report on demonstration last night attached.

ACTION.   See over.   Lt.Colonel,
                            Commanding

ACTION Time		Battery	Target	Rounds	Remarks
From	To				

Program carried out. Fire was opened by request of infantry. In addition —

9 pm		47	Ryans Keep	6	
8.25 pm		59S	A 22 c ½ 7½	9	
3.45 am	4 am	9	Trenches	20	
10 am	10.30 a	9	A22 a 5.4	12	germans leaving to
3.30 pm	3.40 p	9	A22 c 5.6	7	movements
11 am		15	Low farm	38	
10.30 pm		15	Madagascar	18	
2 am	2.40 am	17	Trenches	40	
3.45	4.15 am	17	"	49	
11 am		17			Retaliation
7.45	8 am	47	A 27 D	8	
10.50	11 am				
1 am	4 am	48	night lines	63	"

Rodd
Adj. 41? Bde.

DIARY

DATE 22/12/15

OBSERVATION CONDITIONS. Misty all day observation best 8 - 9 A.M. Possible to 1000 yards behind German line 7 AM 4 PM

WORK DONE BY ENEMY. Nil

MOVEMENT SEEN. Nil

GUNS LOCATED OR SUSPECTED. NIL.

WORKING PARTIES SEEN. NIL.

GENERAL. 11 AM - 1 PM Enemy shelled GIVENCHY heavily with FIELD GUNS. About 1.15 PM to-day Enemy's 4" H.V gun dropped four shells short into German lines between FALSE CULVERT and CANAL During last nights operations The Enemy opened a fairly heavy Rifle and M.G fire from 8 to 8.15 PM. After that there was some more sniping than usual Their Artillery shelled our support trenches CUINCHY HARLEY ST & PONT FIXE 8.15 PM to 11 PM. Quiet until 2.15 PM Our Trenches CAMBRIN and BRADDELL PT were shelled with field guns. This was repeated at 4 PM Total losses inflicted on us on whole A group front are reported as one killed and one wounded.

ACTION. See over.

Lt.Colonel,
Commanding

B Quiller Couch
Lieut & Adjt
A Group

ACTION Time From	To	Battery	Target	Rounds	Remarks
8.15 PM	5 AM	16	CME trenches and 2ND line	173	Retaliation
8.36 PM		71	PLAIN ALLEY	12	"
8.40 PM	9.7 PM	56	Support trenches	30	"
8.15 PM	4.15 AM	50	CME Trenches	240	"
10.30 AM		56	CANAL TRENCH	6	"
"		71	" "	20	"
10.35	10.55	16	A 22 a 5.5	12	"
11 AM		56	TRAIN	12	"
11 AM	1 PM	71	A 17 a 5.5 & CANTELEUX	60	"
2 PM		71	SNIPERS POSTION N BANK	20	Sniper firing at Towpath
"		56	CANAL FORT & EMBANKMENT REDOUBT	70	Retaliation

2nd Divisional Artillery
HOSTILE FIRE REPORT.

22nd December, 1915.

1. GENERAL INFORMATION.

8-0 a.m. flashes seen 90 deg. and 100 deg. mag. from A 20 d 5 6½.
There was singularly little retaliation to our display last night, and as far as one could see what there was, was only 77 mm. on Z2 SIMS KEEP and ZO.

2. HOSTILE FIRE.

No.	Time From	To	Nature	Direction from	Area shelled	Remarks
1.	2-50a		77 mm.	-	CAMBRIN	) about
	3-45a	4-30a	77 mm.	-	- do -	) 40 rounds.
2.	2-50a)		77 mm. or	AUCHY	Road.	Very close to A & Z who took refuge in the cellars.
	4-0 a)		105 mm. gun			
3.	7-30a	8-0a	77 mm.	-	A 27 d	8 rounds.
4.	10-30a		77 mm.	AUCHY	2 & 3 Brick-stacks.	
5.	10-50a	11-0a	105 mm. How.	-	A 25 d	4 rounds.
6.	11-0 a		4.2"	-	KINGSCLERE & WOBURN ABBEY	
7.	10-20a	3-30p	77 mm. H.E.	VIOLAINES & CANTELEUX	GIVENCHY	400 rounds
8.	12-20p	1-0p	105 mm. How. 77 mm. gun.	-	A 27 d	Moderately heavy fire.
9.	12-30p	1-30p	4" Naval	-	HOLLOW & Trenches near CANAL.	
10.	2-5p		8"(?)	-	G 8 a 3 9	4 rounds.
11.	5-30p	5-45p	4" gun	?	41st Brigade mess & vicinity.	No direct hits as yet. 12 Rounds.

Major, R.A.,
Brigade Major, R.A.2/Divn.

DAILY AMMUNITION RETURN

DATE 22nd Decr. 1915

BATTERIES.

Piece	Projectile	Code	50	70	15	48	71	9	16	17	47	56	Total	Per Piece
18-pr	Guns.......													
	Shrapnel...	"A"	186	38	67	248	25	212	202	216			1194	
	H. E.......	"Ax"	55	245	42	83	39	41	135	180			570	
4.5"	Howitzers..													
	Shrapnel...	"B"												
	H. E.......	"Bx"									30	136	166	

Scout

COPY No. 12.

2nd Divisional Artillery Operation Order No. 11.

22nd December, 1915.

Reference 36c N.W. Sheet 1.

A night firing scheme will be carried out by the Artillery of the Corps on a date to be notified later.

2. The tasks and objects of the Divisional Artillery will be as follows :-
   (a) Object:- To cause loss to reliefs and supply personnel and to hinder the distribution of ammunition and rations.

UNIT	TIME	TARGET	AMMUNITION	REMARKS
"A" Group 3 18-pr. Batteries	5-0 p.m. to 8-0 p.m. 5-6 7-8 10-11	PLAIN ALLEY TOWPATH ALLEY CANAL both banks LA BASSEE Road MILL ALLEY	50 rounds per battery 50% H.E.	Search 500 yards to 1500 yards behind enemy's front line.
"Z" Group 4 18-pr. Batteries	-do-	CHATEAU ALLEY DOCK ALLEY AUCHY ALLEY MINE ALLEY CEMETERY ALLEY PEKIN ALLEY HAISNES-AUCHY Road	-do-	Short sharp bursts of fire at irregular intervals. -do-

   (b) Object:- To disturb the enemy's rest, and to cause some personnel to quit the shelter of houses, thus exposing themselves to field gun fire.

UNIT	TIME	TARGET	AMMUNITION	REMARKS
4.5" howitzer 1 Section	1-0 a.m. to 1-3 a.m.	Houses about A 16 d 9½ 0	5 rounds per gun	
2 Sections	-do-	A U C H Y	-do-	
1 Battery	-do-	H A I S N E S	-do-	
"A" Group. 1 18-pr. Battery.	1-5 a.m. to 1-8 a.m.	LA BASSEE Road near A 16 d 9½ 0	20 rounds per battery	50% H.E.
2 18-pr. Batteries	-do-	All roads in A U C H Y	-do-	
"Z" Group. 4 18-pr. Batteries.	-do-	All roads in H A I S N E S	-do-	

please return soon as this copy is borrowed

(2).

(c) Object:- To cause loss to early morning reliefs, 5-0 a.m. till light enough to see.

Repeat as in (a).

Major, R.A.,

Brigade Major, R.A., 2nd Divn.

Issued at   to:-

COPY No. 1. "A" Group.
  ,,   2. "Z" Group.
  ,,   3. 44th Brigade.
  ,,   4. 34th Brigade.
  ,,   5. D.A.C.
  ,,   6 & 7. 2nd Division   )
  ,,   8. H.A., 1st Corps.   )
  ,,   9. R.A., 12th Division) For information.
  ,,   10. R.A., 47th Division)
  ,,   11. 59th Siege   )

1/. Report on Gas attack on night 21-22.

On the previous night 20-21 Gas was let off in A2 subsection.

1. On both occasions Germans visibly lighted fires

Between LA BASSEE Road & Brickstacks there were 4 but it was difficult to distinguish whether in front line or Support Line. Several on Embankment and along CANAL TRENCH and TORTOISE. No fire was lighted between N.E. Brickstack and Embankment. Germans visible in open on Embankment.

2. Machine guns opened fire from just S. of LA BASSEE Road BRICKSTACKS. (CULVERT A.16.c.5½.7) and a point

of between A.16.C.2½.8 and A.16.C.0.8½.

3. Very little rifle fire, and this was over in half an hour. After that there was a good deal of sniping.

4. Red lights sent up, probably calling for Artillery support. On the first occasion the guns did not open for 20 minutes and on the second for 10 mins. The shelling was then heavy on support trenches 77.M.M & 5.9 Hows.

A Patrol sent out by night Battn reported that the Germans appeared unaffected by gas.

It would appear that the two trenches between N.E. Broadstairs & Embankment on our left have been going on here for some time and no fires a seen in these trenches—

3.

2. Opportunities occur for the
    or rifle fire
   Guns & directly the Gas starts as
   the Enemy appear to get ?
   out of their trenches to lighter
   fires. Rifle fire would not
           disperse the Gas.
                    H. Ward Lt Col.

22.12.15.

Report from O.C. 56th
        attached —

Report on night operations.
20th-21st & 21st-22nd Dec.

A. 20th-21st. 10.15 pm. Moderate machine gun fire opened by enemy chiefly N of CANAL. One machine gun located on EMBANKMENT 20x N.W of CULVERT.

10.16 pm A fire appeared on EMBANKMENT redoubt followed almost immediately by two more at the same place & then about 10 more along CANAL TRENCH & TORTOISE.

10.25 – 11.15 pm. 105 cm How from direction of VIOLAINES fired at slow rate on our trenches N of CANAL.

10.30 pm Two red lights sent up from EMBANKMENT REDOUBT.

10.40 – 11.5 pm 77 mm from direction of AUCHY fired on trenches in A2.

At intervals a small searchlight was seen in enemy's lines N of CANAL probably in 3o line trench.

Everything normal by 11.45 pm.

B. 21ˢᵗ–22ⁿᵈ. 8.6 pm Finis lighted in enemy's front
line from N.E brickstack southwards &
on EMBANKMENT REDOUBT but not between
these points.

    8.10 pm 77 mm opened fire on A2
trencher.

    8.18 pm 105 mm opened fire on A1 trencher

    8.25 pm 77 mm batteries from N⁺ᵈ of
LA BASSEE opened fire at A1 & A2 trencher

    8.25 pm 105 mm opened fire on support
& communication trencher just N⁺ᵈ of CANAL

    8.26 pm 77 mm fired at CUINCHY

    8.30 pm 77 mm fired at PONT FIXE

    8.30 – 8.50 pm 150 mm fired a few rounds
on A2 communication trencher from direction
of VIOLAINES.

    9.15 pm all quiet.

    12.0 mn. 77 mm fired a few rounds
to left of A2 section.

    4.0 am. 77 mm fired at A2 trencher &
105 mm at PONT FIXE. ceased at 4.10 am.

    8.22 pm Powerful searchlight on
EMBANKMENT near S. apex of triangle.

General remarks. Almost all fire appeared to come
from the EMBANKMENT, no rifle fire between
CULVERT + N.E. brickstack, these trenches do
not appear to be held except possibly by isolated

posts. No lights were seen to go up from them, & no fires were lighted.

A large number of red lights were sent up either on a S.O. the main road from 8.5pm onwards & one or two were seen N of the CANAL.

A rocket bursting into about 8 white stars was seen at 9.5pm about the EMBANKMENT

22.12.18.

Operations on 2 front night of 21/22 Dec 1915
as viewed from Ridge House.

The enemy appeared to take no alarm till about 8.10. At that time he began sending up more Very lights, & his rate of rifle fire increased, becoming fairly heavy. The Very lights showed up the cloud of gas.

About 8.15 fires were lit on the parapet opposite our trenches between La Bassée Road & Gun Street (as near as could be identified), & a few red & green lights went up opposite Z1.

About this time a search light appeared for about 2 mins from direction of Les Briques.

Z0 & Z2 did not appear to take alarm till about 8.25, & then a few red lights were sent up, & a few fires appeared near junction of Z0 & Z1.

All batteries kept in touch with the front line & fired as desired by the infantry.

The German Artillery commenced about 8.20, mostly opposite Z2 & later near Boyau 9 & Z0.

From a spectators point of view, after 8.30, everything seemed quiet, except slight Artillery fire. The enemy sent up no more lights & (except for one machine gun) firing practically ceased. This machine gun stopped five minutes later.

It appeared the enemy was either asphyxiated or had come to the conclusion there was to be no attack. This is not borne out by the infantry in the trenches, so there must have been some rifle fire that could not be heard from Ridge House.

About 9.15, rifle fire began again to become brisk.

From 2 am to 2.30 am the enemy fired with guns on Com Trenches & on Cambrin & there was some rifle & machine gunfire.

About 4.30 am this was repeated for 20 mins.

M Powell
Lt Col
C 41st Bde R.F.A

DIARY

DATE 23/12/15

OBSERVATION CONDITIONS. Moderate light strong and gusty S.W. wind. Observation possible 7.15 AM – 4 PM.

WORK DONE BY ENEMY. A small new false Hedge has been erected about A 11 C 1.7 either as a screen for men walking on the road or to conceal sniper gun position.

MOVEMENT SEEN. NIL

GUNS LOCATED OR SUSPECTED. NIL

WORKING PARTIES SEEN. NIL

GENERAL. GIVENCHY was heavily shelled last night and again intermittently all day. 300, 77 m.m. shells are reported to have been fired on CHEYNE WALK alone. The majority of the shell fire has been from 77 m.m. guns but a considerable number of 5.9" and 4.2" were fired on the Trenches N of DUCK'S BILL last night. The 4" H.V. guns and 77 m.m. also fired along N canal bank as far as PONT FIXE. The Area between HUN VIEW and KINGSCLERE is becoming very unhealthy owing to the movement there in the day time. Lamp Signalling stations have been tested with good results with a view to carrying out CORPS instructions.

B Guiller Couch.
Lieut & Adjt
for Lt. Colonel,
Commanding A Group

ACTION. See over.

ACTION Time From	To	Battery	Target	Rounds	Remarks
9 PM	11 PM	71	LORGIES ROAD CANAL TRENCH	130	Co-operation with 12TH DIV
9.15 PM	.	50	CANTELEUX ALLEY South & CME Trenches	60	" " "
9.20 PM	-	16	A 22 a 2.8	14	Retaliation.
5 AM		50	CANAL TRENCH	20	Reply to organized
		71	EMBANKMENT REDOUBT	20	German Retaliation.
10.15 AM		16	A 16 d 2½.0	8	Retaliation
11.15	12	56	A 11 C 1.7 & NE BRICKSTACK	28	"
11.15		71	SNIPERS POST CANAL FORT	30	At request of Infantry
1 PM	2 PM	50	EMBANKMENT REDOUBT	40	Retaliation
1.20	2.12P	56	C Brickstack & Train	28	"
1.15		16	Roads in AUCHY	20	Registration
1.15	2.12	71	CANTELEUX & A 17 a 6.7	40	Retaliation
2.30		56	EMBANKMENT	8	"
3.20	3.45	16	A 16 d 1.0	22	"
4 PM		50	AUCHY STATION	20	"

Last night the gas moved across to Enemy's trenches quickly and appeared to reach them before he lit his fires. Many fires were subsequently lit and Red rockets were fired. These gas attacks appear to annoy him considerably if they do nothing else.
A fairly heavy M.G. fire was opened from Ducks Bill where Enemy had at least three M.Gs
9.15 PM to 10 PM considerable artillery fire and after 10 PM intermittent artillery fire until 5 AM when there was an organized bombardment. Enemy apparently expects a raid or attack to follow gas attack just before Daylight.

Z DIARY

DATE 23-12-15

OBSERVATION CONDITIONS.
Possible at 7.30 am. Good.

WORK DONE BY ENEMY.
Some work near Lone Farm.

MOVEMENT SEEN.
A few germans near 'Straw stack' in open.
One german running in front of Auchy.

GUNS LOCATED OR SUSPECTED.

WORKING PARTIES SEEN.

GENERAL.
A train was seen on La Bassée Douvrin Line going South at 7.30 am and 11.40 am.

ACTION. See over.

F. Rodd
Adj.
for Commanding Lt. Colonel, Z group

ACTION Time From	To	Battery	Target	Rounds	Remarks
9.30pm	22 12/15	15	Madagascar Tr	12	Iz request
8 am	23 12/15	17	Wartwig park	4	
8.30 am		17	" "	9	
9.20		17	Germans in open	8	as reported
9.30	9.40	9	A 22 b 7.8	25	Suspected OP
10.35	11.45	17	Low farm. tr.	55	
11 am		59	A16a 5½·0 A16c 2·9	15	registration
11.50 am		17	ETNA	42	retaliation
12.20 pm		47	Ryans keep	5	
12.20 pm		9	A 22 a 5.6	29	"
1.45 pm	3.30 pm	17	Trenches	50	"
1.55	2.5	9	"	18	"
2.45	3.50	15	Madagascar t.	55	"
3.15		47	Ryans keep	4	" to minnie
3.22		47	" "	16	" "
3.30	3.45	9	Auchy	42	"
3.50 pm		17	Trenches	6	Instruction
11.35 pm	22 12/15	48	night lines mine pt.	45	retaliation
1.45 am		48	Auchy mine pt	32	"
14.5 am		71	Railway t	30	"
2 pm	4.30 pm	48	Auchy mine pt & t	47	"

2nd Divisional Artillery

HOSTILE FIRE REPORT.

23rd December, 1915.

1. GENERAL INFORMATION.

Observation possible 7-15 a.m.- 4-0 p.m. Gas attack north of CANAL last night caused much retaliation. GIVENCHY and O.M.E. trenches being bombarded intermittently all night and again to-day. CHEYNE Walk came in for particular attention. Gas went across to enemy's lines well, and got there apparently before his fires were lit.

Train was seen moving along railway LA BASSEE-DOUVRIN LINE, towards DOUVRIN at 7-30 a.m. and 11-40 a.m.

2. HOSTILE FIRE.

No.	Time From	To	Nature	Direction from	Area shelled	Remarks.
1.	22nd 9-30p	7-0a	5.9" & 77 mm.	VIOLAINES	CHEYNE WALK FRONT LINE	300 rds of 77 mm. were fired at CHEYNE WALK alone.
2.	11-30p		77 mm.	A U C H Y	Z 1	15 rds.
3.	23rd 1-0a	1-30a	4" H Y guns	LA BASSEE	O M E Trenches HUN VIEW KINGSCLERE	40 rds
4.	1-45a		4.2"	HAISNES	MAISON ROUGE	12 rds
5.	9-15a		77 mm.	,,	,, ,,	6 rds
6.	10-0a	12noon	,,		GIVENCHY	100 rds
7.	11-40a		,,	-	BRADDELL POINT & BOYAU 19.	8 rds
8.	12noon	12-10p	4" H Y guns		PONT FIXE N. CANAL BANK.	40 rds
9.	1-5 p	1-20p	77 mm.		HUN VIEW	
10.	1-20p		5.9"		In front of "400"	5 rds
11.	2-0p Intermittently	4-30p	4.2" & 77 mm.	A U C H Y	Z1 & Z0	80 rds
12.	2-10p	2-25p	105 mm.		CUINCHY	20 rds
13.	2-45p	2-50p	77 mm.		HOLLOW	20 rds
14.	3-20p		4.2"How.	-	E.of MOUNTAIN HOUSE.	?
15.	3-20p		,,	A U C H Y	MAISON ROUGE	?
16.	11-45a & 2-30p		4.2"	-	CROSS ROAD VERMELLES.	40 rds
17.	All afternoon		77 mm.		GIVENCHY	Intermittent.

Major, R.A.,
Brigade Major, R.A., 2/Divn.

DAILY AMMUNITION RETURN

DATE 23rd Dec. 1915

BATTERIES

Piece	Projectile	Code	50	70	15	48	71	9	16	17	47	56	Total Per Piece
18-pr	Guns.......												
	Shrapnel...	"A"	102	33	32	100	110	34	22	95			528
	H.E.......	"Ax"	13	117	15	16	88	41	14	80			384
4.5"	Howitzers..												
	Shrapnel...	"B"											
	H.E.......	"Bx"										81	81

"A" Form. Army Form C. 2121.
MESSAGES AND SIGNALS.

Prefix	Code	m.	Words	Charge	This message is on a/c of :	Recd. at	m.
Office of Origin and Service Instructions.			Sent			Date	
			At	m.	Service.	From	
			To			By	
			By		(Signature of "Franking Officer.")		

TO { A Group
     Z Group

| Sender's Number | Day of Month | In reply to Number | AAA |
| BM 971 | 23 | | |

Tomorrow No. 1 Group HAR will bombard Western portion of TRIANGLE with 12" and 15" howitzers aaa If weather is favourable bombardment will commence at 10.30 am aaa OC 18th Battery is in charge of operations aaa He will inform OC A Group at 9 am whether the bombardment will take place or not aaa In event of postponement he will give 1½ hours notice to OC A Group before bombardment starts aaa On hearing from OC A Group the hour at which bombardment will commence GOC 5th Infantry Brigade will arrange to withdraw men as necessary aaa

From
Place
Time

The above may be forwarded as now corrected.   (Z)
                                    Censor.   Signature of Addressor or person authorised to telegraph in his name.
* This line should be erased if not required.

"A" Form.
MESSAGES AND SIGNALS.
Army Form C. 2121.

Prefix	Code	m.	Words	Charge	This message is on a/c of:	Recd. at	m.
Office of Origin and Service Instructions.			Sent			Date	
			At	m.	Service.	From	
			To				
			By		(Signature of "Franking Officer.")	By	

TO

Sender's Number	Day of Month	In reply to Number	AAA

Infantry OC 18th Lucie Barking with
ham OC A Group of the hours at
which the bombardment of the
area and front line can be
reoccupied aaa A Group will
be prepared to cover reoccupation
of firing line by infantry after
heavy bombardment has
ceased aaa acknowledge
aaa

From R.A. 7 Div
Place
Time 4.5 pm

The above may be forwarded as now corrected.   (Z)
* Censor.   Signature of Addressor or person authorised to telegraph in his name.
* This line should be erased if not required.

"A" Form.
MESSAGES AND SIGNALS.
Army Form C. 2121.

Prefix......Code......m.	Words	Charge	This message is on a/c of:	Recd. at.........m.
Office of Origin and Service Instructions.	Sent			Date............
	At......m.		......Service.	From............
	To......			By............
	By......		(Signature of "Franking Officer.")	

TO { A Corps
      Z Corps

| Sender's Number | Day of Month | In reply to Number | AAA |
| BM 972 | 23 | | |

In addition to bombardment by 12 and 15 inch tr[ench] mor[tars] heavy artillery 1st Corps is bombarding A/c 44 area with heavy and 6 inch guns. Hour not decided.

From: R.A. 7 Div
Place:
Time: 10.5 p.m.

(Z) Signature of Addresser

2nd Divisional Artillery Orders

by

Brigadier-General G.H.SANDERS, D.S.O., Comdg.R.A., 2nd Division.

23rd December,1915.

1198. R.A.ORDERS.

Were not issued Tuesday, 21st Decr., and Wednesday,22nd Decr.,1915.

1199. HEADCOVER.

There are at present no more poles at W.21.c. Notice will be given as soon as more can be obtained.
There is still plenty of brushwood for windscreens.

1200. RETURNS.

All units will report to this Office by the evening of 25th: instant the number of (a) Roman Catholics (b) Presbyterians (c) Wesleyans and Free Church Officers and Other Ranks under their command.

1201. COOKS.

Thoroughly efficient and energetic master cooks are required as instructors by the Division. OsC., Brigades will please send names of any men whom they recommend to this office by midday 26th:instant.

L.G.BUXTON,Capt,R.A.,
Staff Captain, R.A.,2nd Divn.

DIARY

DATE 24/12/15

OBSERVATION CONDITIONS. Light good except during the rain showers which were fairly frequent throughout the day. Wind S.W strong and gusty. Observation possible 7.15 AM to 3.45 PM

WORK DONE BY ENEMY. None observed

MOVEMENT SEEN. 10 AM Four men seen walking behind Train on S.W of Triangle.
3.30 PM movement seen behind trenches A 23 b 3 9

GUNS LOCATED OR SUSPECTED. Nil

WORKING PARTIES SEEN. 9.5 AM Enemy were seen working near NE Brickstack work stopped when fired on.
11 AM FALSE CULVERT two men seen.

GENERAL. The enemy have been quiet all day from 8 AM
7 AM to 8 AM. There was much activity. AT 7.15 we exploded a mine near the CHORD of HOHENZOLLERN and enemy blew a mine north of DUCKS BILL at almost exactly the same time. Both mines were followed by a sharp bombardment on both sides. Damage done by mines not being on our front has not been reported.

B. Quille Couch
Lieut & Adjt
for
Lt. Colonel,
Commanding 'A' Group.

ACTION. See over.

ACTION Time		Battery	Target	Rounds	Remarks
From	To				
7.15A	7.30	16	2ND line North of ROAD	55	Retaliation for mine
		71	CANAL TRENCH	40	
7.30		50	EMBANKMENT FORT	45	"
7.40		56	TORTOISE	30	"
9.10		"	NE Brickstack	12	Working Party
10AM		16	TRAIN	6	Movement seen
11.20	12.20	71	CANAL TRENCH	40	Retaliation
12.15	2.30	50	WATER & Embankment fort	39	"
1.10	2.22	56	CANAL HOUSE	33	"
2.30		56	HOUSE in CANTELEAX	13	Suspected O P
1PM	2.30	71	TORTOISE & A17a 67	60	Retaliation
3.30		16	A 23 & 3.9	8	Movement seen
4 PM		50	Canal Tow path	12	Checked lines for night firing

Z DIARY

DATE 24-12-15

OBSERVATION CONDITIONS. Possible 7.20. Good.

WORK DONE BY ENEMY.
No fresh work observed.

MOVEMENT SEEN. Men seen moving in to in front of La Bosques almost railway in front of Auchy. ✗

GUNS LOCATED OR SUSPECTED.
Flashes suspected from A.30.d at 2pm but very doubtful.

WORKING PARTIES SEEN.
Men carrying timber A.29.b.3.7 wearing (one cap blue jersey or tunic white breeches and knee boots!

GENERAL.
Smoke from houses in Auchy.
The two mines in Hohenzollern went up 7.07 am but the two flashes were almost simultaneous. About 30 to 60s later the Germans fired three red lights. 48th and 47th opened fire simultaneously with 6th (Div) Div R.F.A.

ACTION.   See over.

                                    [signature] adj.
                                    Lt.Colonel,
                                    Commanding Group.

ACTION Time From	To	Battery	Target	Rounds	Remarks
7.45pm		47	Roads &c	8	retaliation to hmm?
9.30pm		47	Houses	18	
7.18am	7.35	48	Hacarburg tr	75	program
7.18am	7.26	71		62	
7.18	7.33	47	A28d 25 to 4.5	50	"
7.20		15	Supports	20	retaliation
7.40	7.50	48	Music pt.	12	"
9.30	9.40	48	"	4	"
12 noon		48	Anghy mounds	8	
12 noon		15	Rd. A20 R.1.0.	15	registration
10.45pm		9	Aucky	20	retaliation
12.15pm		9	Aucky A220 A4	13	movement seen
12.45		9	The men carrying timber		
1.45		15	Madgascar	37	retaliation
2pm		15	Low farm	7	registration
2.12	2.28	47	Aucky	12	suspected O.P.
2.45		9	Party seen sand bagging windows of a house seen	39	
2.45	4pm	48	Low farm	11	registration
3.45		15	town Madgascar	29	retaliation
5pm		15	Madgascar tr	16	"
11.15	12.15	59	A23C	79	
7pm	5am	17	Trenches	49	
7.30am		17	"	37	retaliation
12.15pm		17	"	23	movement

"A" Form.   Army Form C. 2121.

MESSAGES AND SIGNALS.

Prefix	Code	m.	Words	Charge	This message is on a/c of.	Recd. at	m.
Office of Origin and Service Instructions.			Sent At ... m. To ... By ...		Service. (Signature of "Franking Officer.")	Date From By	

TO
- ~~5th Bde~~   ~~1 Corps~~   ~~1 Group HAR~~
- ~~99 Bde~~   ~~12th Div~~
- RA 2Dn   ~~4th Div~~

Sender's Number: G3   Day of Month: 23   In reply to Number: AAA

Reference 2Dn G 991 dated 22nd aaa Bombardment of Western end of TRIANGLE will take place tomorrow if weather is suitable commencing at 10.30 am aaa First warning to OC A group 2Dn RA and front line troops at 9 am aaa Otherwise all arrangements hold good for tomorrow as made for today aaa Addressees 5th 99th Bdes RA 2Dn Repeated Corps. 12th and 4th Divs and 1st group HAR

Rec'd 4.10pm
23/12/15

(Priority)

From: 2Dn
Place:
Time: 3.40pm

B. Belgrave
Major

2nd Divisional Artillery

HOSTILE FIRE REPORT.

24th December, 1915.

1. GENERAL INFORMATION.

Observation possible at 7-15 a.m.

2. HOSTILE FIRE.

No.	Time From	To	Nature	Direction From	Area shelled	Remarks
1.	7-15a		4.2"H.E.	-	DUCKS BILL	10 rds on explosion of mine.
2.	7-20a	7-50a	77 mm.) 105 mm.) How.)	?	(Z2 (LA BASSEE - (VERMELLES Rd	Retaliation by Germans - 250 rds.
3.	7-25a	8-0a	4.2"H.E.	-	Trenches N.of CANAL BRICKFIELDS & KINGSCLERE	
4.	7-40a		77 mm.		ORCHARD FARM	25 rds.
5.	8-0a	9-0a	,,	AUCHY	A 20 b 8 2	30 rds.
6.	10-45a		,,	AUCHY	CAMBRIN E.	6 rds.
7.	11-20a	12-30p	,,		ORCHARD FARM	25 rds.
8.	12noon	2-30p	77 mm. 4.2"H.E. 5.9"H.E.		CANAL BANK and all trenches in A2 ORCHARD FARM	In retaliation to Heavy's bombardment enemy fire intense between 1-30p & 2-0p
9.	1-45p		105 mm. How.	VIOLAINES	BURBURE	10 rds.

Major, R.A.,

Brigade Major, R.A., 2nd Divn.

DAILY AMMUNITION RETURN

DATE 24th Dec. 1915

BATTERIES.

Piece	Projectile	Code	50	70	15	48	71	9	16	17	47	56	Total Por Piece
18-pr	Guns......												
	Shrapnel...	"A"	88	10	76	157	37	33	81	72			554
	H. E......	"Ax"	78	84	20	116	117	82	37	136			670
4.5"	Howitzers..												
	Shrapnel...	"B"									2		2
	H. E......	"Bx"									107	114	221

2nd Divisional Artillery Orders

by

Brigadier-General G.H.SANDERS, D.S.O., Comdg.R.A., 2nd Divn.

24th December, 1925.

1202. GUNS & HOWITZERS.- BUFFERS OF

 Buffer oil begins to thicken at 14° F. and becomes very thick at 7° F.
 If it appears that such low temperatures are likely to be experienced, buffers (when guns are not in action) should be covered with sandbags filled with straw. This should be sufficient to prevent oil falling to the temperatures mentioned above.

L.G.BUXTON, Capt, R.A.,

Staff Captain, R.A., 2nd Divn.

Z DIARY

DATE 25-12-15

OBSERVATION CONDITIONS.

Observation good.

WORK DONE BY ENEMY.

MOVEMENT SEEN. Some germans seen near 3 Cabarets and Love farm.
Smoke seen from house in Auchy. Treated with H.E.

GUNS LOCATED OR SUSPECTED.

WORKING PARTIES SEEN. Same party seen sandbagging house in Corons as yesterday.

GENERAL.
The same german described yesterday carrying timber was again seen today. He had the same breeches and boots on but another tunic and cap. This man is always being seen here also always carrying wood.
Another german was seen today with a green french cloth cap on.

ACTION.   See over.

Rodd
Lt. Colonel,
Commanding Z Group.

ACTION

Time From	To	Battery	Target	Rounds	Remarks
At night		programme as ordered			
8.45 pm		9	A23 c07 House		smoke
11 am		9	A23 a 0.6 Rd.		party moving
12 noon		9	CORONS A19a15		party sandbagging house
2 pm		9	Trenches		by request
3.50		9	"		"
8.45 am		17	Auchy	9	retaliation
11.20		17	Germans	9	
2.45	3 pm	17	Lone farm	20	work
3.43	4.17	17	Germans	5	
11.47 pm		47	Ryan heap	4	retaliation to mine
9.30 am		47	A29b	4	germans
10.25		47	Les Barques	10	a fire
2 pm		47	Trenches	8	retaliation
12 mid.		15	Madagascar	2	retaliation
3.10 pm		15	"	22	"
3.45		15	Railway Cott.	13	registration
4 pm		15	Madagascar	16	retaliation
3.30 p	4.3	48	Trenches	18	
2.45 pm		59	Ryan heap	10	retaliation

DIARY

DATE 25/12/15

OBSERVATION CONDITIONS. Light good between showers. Wind S.W. gusty. Observation possible 7AM to 4PM.

WORK DONE BY ENEMY. Nothing new to report

MOVEMENT SEEN. Enemy seen moving along 2ND line trench in TORTOISE 12.45 Probably a carrying party with Dinners

GUNS LOCATED OR SUSPECTED. 5.9" Battery firing on LE PREOL 5 II C 5.0 gave very visible flashes between 3.40 and 4 PM. These were at a true Bearing of 71 degrees from A.15 c 2.8. This might give comparisons with guns suspected by Divisions on our left.

WORKING PARTIES SEEN.
10.30 AM A21 6 9.7.
1.30 PM   A 22 6 3.9.

GENERAL. The enemy have been fairly quiet. There was only some shelling of CHEYNE WALK in reply to our night firing. Night firing times have been altered to ensure the enemy being unprepared. VILLAGE HATE will be 9.30 - 9.38 PM.
MORNING " 6 - 8 AM
5.9" Battery firing on LE PREOL this afternoon were almost certainly trying for Battery F16 d 8.4. No damage was apparently done. An engine with a very unusual whistle has been constantly heard from BETHUNE. The Blasts are given in dots and dashes and OP's report that the noise as heard there is very similar to a BUZZER. This was also heard last night.

ACTION. See over.

B Quiller Couch
Lieut & Adj for
Lt.Colonel,
Commanding A Group.

| ACTION Time | | Battery | Target | Rounds | Remarks |
From	To				
8 PM	11 PM	16	Fired as per	120	
1	1.8 AM	50	OPERATION	120	
		70	ORDER No. 11	100	
5 AM	7 AM	56		30	
8.30	8.50 A	16	2nd line Trenches	14	Retaliation
8.50	9.5	56	TRAIN	21	"
9 AM		71	A 15 d 8.9	30	SNIPER'S Active on Tow Path
10.30	10.50	16	A 21 b 9.7	10	Working Party
11.15		50	Houses in TRIANGLE	20	Smoke Seen
12.45	12.55	56	TORTOISE	6	Movement seen
1.30	1.45	16	A 22 b 3.9	22	Working Party
2.45		16	2nd line	8	Enemy firing at our Aeroplanes
3.15	3.25	56	NE Brickstack	6	"

2nd Divisional Artillery

Hostile Fire Report.

25th December, 1915.

1. GENERAL INFORMATION.

Flashes of 5.9" How. Battery shelling LE PREOL neighbourhood gave very visible flashes 3-40 to 4-0p.m. to-day. True bearing 71 degrees from HUN VIEW.

2. HOSTILE FIRE.

No.	Time From	Time To	Nature	Direction from	Area shelled	Remarks.
	24th.					
1.	10-0p	10-30p	77 mm.	?	CHEYNE WALK	
	25th.					
2.	7-0a		4.2" & 77 mm.		GIVENCHY	
3.	8-25a)	8-45a	105 mm. How.	HAISNES	(A 21 b (vicinity BRADDELL (POINT	7 rds.
4.	8-40a)					
5.	8-50a	9-5a	5.9"	?	CUINCHY	
6.	8-50a		5.9"		GIVENCHY	only 6 rds.
7.	9-40a	9-50a	4.2"	HAISNES	PONT FIXE	
8.	9-55a	10-0a	77 mm.	?	HARLEY Street	
9.	11-30a		,,	LA BASSEE	ANNEQUIN	
10.	1-45p	2-5p	150 mm.	?	A 27 a	12 rds.
11.	1-15p	2-0p	105 mm.	?	F 29 d	10 rds.
12.	4-0p	5-0p	4" gun	LA BASSEE	ANNEQUIN	
13.	4-23p	4-40p	105 mm.	?	ANNEQUIN S.	20 rds.

Major, R.A.,
Brigade Major, R.A., 2nd Division.

[1647]

DAILY AMMUNITION RETURN

DATE 25th Decr. 1915

Piece	Projectile	Code	BATTERIES.										Total Per Piece
			50	70	15	48	71	9	16	17	47	56	
18-pr	Guns......												
	Shrapnel...	"A"	72	41	49	78	70	171	79	78			638
	H. E.......	"Ax"	149	114	44	103	90	205	91	96			892
4.5"	Howitzers..												
	Shrapnel...	"B"									—	—	—
	H. E.......	"Bx"									63	158	221

2nd Divisional Artillery Orders

by

Brigadier-General G.H.SANDERS, D.S.O., Comdg.R.A., 2nd Divn.

25th December, 1915.

1203. TUBE HELMETS.

As units have now been completed with the 2nd Tube Helmet, they should return without delay the ordinary film-eyepiece (Hypo)Helmets thus released.

1204. FIELD SERVICE BOOTS.

Indents are to be submitted to D.A.D.O.S. by the undermentioned units for the number of pairs of F.S.Boots shown against each:-

R.A., Brigade Headquarters.,............... each 3 pairs.
Batteries, R.F.A......................... each 5 pairs.
Bde.Ammunition Columns................... each 5 pairs.
2nd Divisional Ammunition Column......... 15 pairs.

1205. DIVINE SERVICE.

Services will be held to-morrow, 26th instant, as under:-

(a) CHURCH OF ENGLAND.
3-0 p.m............ In the Divisional Concert Hall, RUE D'AIRE, taken by Bishop GWYNNE, Deputy Chaplain General, for all R.F.A., Units.

7 a.m. and 8 a.m........ Holy Communion.

6-0 p.m. Voluntary Service, followed by Concert.

(b) ROMAN CATHOLICS.
10-30 a.m................BETHUNE Cathedral.

1206. COURTMARTIAL.

A F.G.C.M., will assemble at Headquarters, R.A., 2nd Divn. (18 RUE SADI-CARNOT, BETHUNE) at 10-0 a.m. on Monday 27th Decr., 1915 for the trial of No.39337, Br.Hill.J., 50th Bty.R.F.A., No.55234, Dr. Chesterton.H.G., 50th Bty.R.F.A., No.14029, Dr. McCormick.W:-

PRESIDENT.
Major T.N.FRENCH.   -   47th Battery, R.F.A.

MEMBERS.
Captain E.W.GRIFFITH. -   44th B. A. C.
Lieutenant H.LOWE.   -   9th Battery, R.F.A.

The accused to be warned and all witnesses duly required to attend.
Proceedings to be forwarded to Staff Captain, R.A. 2nd Division.
Court Orderly to be supplied by 34th Brigade, R.F.A.

L.G.BUXTON, Capt, R.A.,
Staff Captain, R.A., 2nd Division.

DIARY

1649

DATE 26/12/15

OBSERVATION CONDITIONS. Observation possible 7.30 AM 4 PM. Wind SW moderate and showery. Light fair all day.

WORK DONE BY ENEMY. Nothing new observed.

MOVEMENT SEEN.
9.55 AM Seven of the enemy walking in open from CANTELEUX towards A 17 a 5.7

11 35 AM A 16 a 2.6 enemy seen looking over their trench

9.10 AM Enemy waving handkerchiefs in Embankment Redoubt.

GUNS LOCATED OR SUSPECTED. Nil

WORKING PARTIES SEEN. 8.30 AM men digging near railway A 22 b 2.9

GENERAL. The enemy have been quiet during past 24 hours and shelling has been confined to a few odd rounds here and there. Their 4.2 Hows were more active than usual particularly in neighbourhood of KINGSCLERE and LOCK.

ACTION. See over.

B Quilter Couch
Lieut & Adjt
for Lt.Colonel,
Commanding A group.

ACTION Time From	To	Battery	Target	Rounds	Remarks
5 PM	11 PM	50 71 16	Enemys Communications	50 50 50	
9.30	9.33 PM	56	AUCHY	30	Christmas "HATE"
9.35	9.38	16 50	" "	20 20	
6 AM	8 AM	50 71 16	Enemys Communications	50 50 50	
8.30 A		16	A.22 b 2.9	9	Working party
10.30	11.30	71	CANTELEUX and A 18 a	50	Retaliation
11.35	11.50	56	EMBANKMENT REDOUBT & A16 a 2.6	24	Movement seen
11.50		50	Embankment Redoubt	20	Retaliation
12.30	1.45 PM	71	M.G. Emplacement A 16 a 2.5	25	Overhead cover and position blown in
			House A11 c 1½.6 where smoke was seen	25	3 direct hits
3.30 PM		16	Iron tank A16 d 5.7	8	Retaliation
"		56	Embankment Redoubt	18	For shelling of LOCK

DAILY DIARY   Z. Group. RA.

DATE 26.12.15.

OBSERVATION CONDITIONS. Possible at 7.35 am, good all day until 4.20 pm.

WORK DONE BY ENEMY.

MOVEMENT SEEN. Several parties of Germans were seen in the open at A22 d 64 and A22 d 5.6.
Men were seen go to & from Corons B 19 a 5½ - 1½ apparently orderlies, they moved behind the buildings.

GUNS LOCATED OR SUSPECTED.

WORKING PARTIES SEEN.
Earth was seen to be thrown out of Book Alley.

GENERAL. A working party was seen at A29 a 92.
At 3 pm 3 lights were observed to be sent up from FOSSE TRENCH.

ACTION.   See over.   Lt. Colonel,
Commanding Group.

ACTION

Time From	To	Battery	Target	Rounds	Remarks
10·10 am	—	9th Batt	German 2nd Line		In retaliation
1·30 pm	—	do	Party of Germans in A 22 d 6 4		
2·15 pm	—	do	do in A 22 d 5 6		
2·30 pm	—	do	Suspected O.P. A 23 a ½ 5		
8·25 am	—	17th Batt	Germans in open	2	
9·40 am	—	do	do	2	
11·40 am	—	do	do	1	
12·30 pm	12·50 pm	do	German Front Line	—	Hostile M.G. fire at one of our aeroplanes.
2·15 pm	—	do	Working Party	12	In from of Straw Stack AUCHY.
2·50 pm	—	do	Front Line	17	Retaliation.
6 am	—	15th Batt	MADAGASCAR TRENCH	4	do
1 pm	3·40 pm	do	do	69	do and keeping down fire on our aeroplanes.
10·50 am	—	47th Batt	Working Party	10	They were dispersed.
9·35 pm	—	48th Batt	HAISNES	20	In retaliation.
12 mid	12·30 am	do	RAILWAY TRENCH	75	do at request of Inf.
9·40 am	10 am	do	AUCHY	20	do
12·40 pm	2·35 pm	do	RAILWAY TRENCH	60	To keep down fire on our aeroplanes.
1·15 pm	3·10 pm	5G S.Batt	A 28 c 4 8 / A 28 a ½ 1½ / A 28 c 10 7 / A 28 a 6 0	28 A.P.	Registration.

All Batteries fired last night according to programme as ordered.

Reeves 2/5
for Adj 41st Bde RFA

2nd Divisional Artillery

HOSTILE FIRE REPORT.

26th December, 1915.

1. GENERAL INFORMATION.

Observation possible 8-0 a.m. to 4-0 p.m.

2. HOSTILE FIRE.

No.	Time From	To	Nature	Direction from	Area shelled	Remarks.
1.	25th. 9-50p		77 mm.		A2 C M E Trenches.	
2.	26th. 9-45a	10-15a	105mm.	A U C H Y	xxxxxxx WILSONS WAY etc.	xxxxxxxxxxxxxxxxxx 3 min. intervals.
3.	10-20a	10-45a	4.2"	LA BASSEE	KINGSCLERE	
4.	10-30a	12noon	77 mm.	A U C H Y	RAILWAY	See below* One gun.
5.	11-30a		,,	?	B1 Trenches.	(Front Line)
6.	11-50a	12noon	4.2"		KINGSCLERE	
7.	11-55a	12-30p	77 mm.	?	A 21 a & b	25 rds.
8.	12-5p		,,		HOLLOW.	
9.	1-55p	2-5p	,,	?	A 27 a	S. of road - 8 rds.
10.	2-20p		,,	VERT	FEUILLAGE-CAMBRIN	6 rds.
11.	3-0p	3-45p	150mm.	HAISNES	A 25 b	35 rds.
12.	3-30p	3-45p	5.9"		N. Bank of CANAL between SPOIL BANK and PONT FIXE	12 rds.

* No.4 was entirely due to Infantry exposing themselves on Railway between HUMANITY and The FACTORY.

Capt, R.A.,
Staff Captain, R.A., 2nd Divn.

DAILY AMMUNITION RETURN

DATE 26th Dec. 1915

BATTERIES.

Piece	Projectile	Code	50	70	15	48	71	9	16	17	47	56	Total	Per Piece
18-pr	Guns......													
	Shrapnel...	"A"	79	1	35	194	36	192	101	68			726*	
	H.E.......	"Ax"	99	161	2	68	114	99	98	84			745*	
4.5"	Howitzers..													
	Shrapnel...	"B"										35		
	H.E.......	"Bx"									38	50	88	
18/pr	Shrapnel	"A"					20*							
H.E (71st Bty detached Sec)		"Ax"					20*							

* Included in total

2nd Divisional Artillery Orders

by

Brigadier-General G.H.SANDERS, D.S.O.,Comdg.R.A.,2nd Divn.

26th December,1915

1207. AMMUNITION-MEN PROCEEDING ON LEAVE.

As, in spite of many warnings on this subject, N.C.Os. and men continue to take their ammunition with them when proceeding on leave, any man found in possession of ammunition at the port of Embarkation on, or after 1st January,1916 when about to proceed on leave will be refused his leave and returned to his unit.

The I.G.C., has been requested to give effect to this order.

1208. RAILHEAD.

Until further notice railhead will be CHOCQUES, from the 27th instant (incl) The hour for reloading will be 10-0a.m. for 2nd Division.

1209. STORES.

After the 2nd Divn.Infantry have moved into rest, units must apply for Ordnance Stores to D.A.D.O.S.,Office on the Quay. D.A.D.O.S., will not be able to supply direct at re-filling point.

1210. TIMBER.- SHORTAGE OF

G.H.Q., have notified that there is a likelihood of a great shortage of timber.

O.C.Brigades will therefore economise as much as possible. For instance, all rifle racks are in future to be made of tin and iron. Notice Boards, number boards and sign posts generally to be also made of tin and iron.

Rabbit netting and brushwood are to be used instead of planking for revetments.

R.A.Units should make arrangements to do without wood as far as possible.

1211. SANDBAGS.

Reference R.A.Circular No.1165, dated 18th instant. Sandbags will in future be sent to the nearest R.E.Store and not to D.A.D.O.S.

L.G.BUXTON, Capt, R.A.,
Staff Captain, R.A., 2nd Divn.

Z DIARY

DATE 27-12-15

1653

OBSERVATION CONDITIONS.

WORK DONE BY ENEMY.

MOVEMENT SEEN. Germans on Hulluch rd at 11.30 a.m. also crossing from Pekin alley to Mad alley about 8 a.m. Some were seen behind Les Briques.

GUNS LOCATED OR SUSPECTED.

WORKING PARTIES SEEN. at A 30 a 8.3 erecting wooden frame, like goal posts on parapet of trench.
About 100 S of Lone farm 11 a.m.

GENERAL. A telephone wire on post near "chateau alley" was cut by 9th Batt.
A tree on Auchy Vermelles road was cut down by german shell 2/15 p.m.
17th Batt fired 61 rds on ETNA group of craters. Sandbags were thrown up and parapet breached in two places. Five or six germans were bolted from one of the craters near our line. The crater to L of St_ x S6 is full of water. It is significant that there was no retaliation.

ACTION. See over.

Rodd
Lt. Colonel,
Commanding Z Group.

ACTION

Time From	To	Battery	Target	Rounds	Remarks
2.30p	3.0p	9	Loophole n.t.	25	demolished "Weekly strong pt"
12. noon	12.30pm	15	Madagascar t.	39	retaliation
9.55am		17	Trenches	3	" "
10.20am		17	A29a 9.5	6	working party
11.35am		17	"	2	" "
3pm	3.30pm	17	Etna craters	61	see report
8.50am		47	A29a 9.3	7	dispersed working party
10.25am		47	A28b 2.5	8	" " "
8.30am	8.38	48	Lone farm	6	" " "
9.30	9.40	48	Mine pt. Popesneek	6	retaliation
12.15pm	12.30	48	Tr. S. Lone farm	12	
12.30	12.35	48	Men on Rly & behind Les Bougies	6	
2pm	2.30pm	48	House A24c57	10	
2.45	3pm	48	Mad alley	2	reregistration
3.30p		48	Mine pt.	4	
4.50	4.55	48	Mine pt etc	30	retaliation + to catch reliefs

55th Siege did not fire.

DIARY

DATE 27/12/15.

OBSERVATION CONDITIONS. Light good wind S.W. half a gale. Observation possible 7.15AM - 4PM.

WORK DONE BY ENEMY. None observed.

MOVEMENT SEEN. Periscopes seen in Embankment Redoubt at 3PM and were fired on.

GUNS LOCATED OR SUSPECTED. NIL.

WORKING PARTIES SEEN. 12.20 PM. Enemy working in their trench A.22.b.3.9.

GENERAL. The enemy set on HUN VIEW at 1PM with 77 m.m HE and after two direct hits on the front wall the third hit caused the front wall to collapse exposing the wood and sandbags. An attempt is being made to night to conceal the exposed work but it is feared that the enemy will probably turn on heavy artillery now that he has seen that it was a fortified O.P.
At present it is destroyed for the purpose of observing.

B. Quiller Couch,
Lieut & Adj.
for Lt. Colonel,
Commanding A Group.

ACTION. See over.

ACTION

Time From	To	Battery	Target	Rounds	Remarks.
8.35A		56	Enemy in Open A 10 d 9.6	15	
10.30		71	CANTELEUX	30	Retaliation
"		56	CANAL HOUSE	24	"
10.45		50	EMBANKMENT	20	"
12.15		71	CANAL TRENCH A16 d 6.9	40	"
12.20		16	A 22 b 3.9	7	Working party
1	2 PM	71	A 17 a 5.5.	60	Retaliation
1.15		50	A 18 a 9.6 WATER TANK	30	Retaliation for shelling COWL HOUSE
1.20		56	EMBANKMENT	26	
2	2.50	16	Enemy's Support Trenches	12	Retaliation
2.20		56	EMBANKMENT	26	"
2.30		71	PT 2.3	20	MG Emplacement
3 PM		50	Embankment	14	Periscope seen.

2nd Divisional Artillery

HOSTILE FIRE REPORT.

27th December, 1915.

HOSTILE FIRE.

No.	Time From	Time To	Nature	Direction from	Area shelled	Remarks.
1	9-0a	9-20a	4" H.V. gun.	LA BASSEE	PONT FIXE	75% Blind.
2.	9-0a	9-30a	4.2"	VIOLAINES	GUNNER Siding	10 rds.
3.	9-52a		77 mm.	A U C H Y	A 21 d trench.	5 rds.
4.	10-10a	11-30a	4.2"	N. of CANAL by LA BASSEE	CANAL TRENCH	30 rds.
5.	10-20a	10-30a	77 mm.		CUINCHY	14 rds.
6.	11-0 a		4.2" & 77 mm.	VIOLAINES	SPOIL BANK	
7.	11-30a	11-45a	105 mm. gun.	?	A 26 b	8 rds.
8.	1-20p	1-45p	5.9"		GIVENCHY	8 rds.
9.	1-30p	2-0p	77 mm.	LA BASSEE	HUN VIEW	OP Destroyed - At any rate temporarily. 40 rds.
10.	1-40p	1-45p	,,	?	A 27 b	4 rds.
11.	1-46p		,,	?	A 25 b 05	3 rds.
12.	2-0p	2-20p	,,	A U C H Y	CHEYNE WALK	10 rds.
13.	2-50p	3-10p	,,		Trenches A1.	20 rds.

Capt, R.A.,
Staff Captain, R.A., 2nd Divn.

1655

DAILY AMMUNITION RETURN

DATE 29th Dec. 1915.

BATTERIES.

Piece	Projectile	Code	50	70	15	48	71	9	16	17	47	56	Total	Per Piece
18-pr	Guns.......													
	Shrapnel...	"A"	—	28	100	43	2	49	22	18			262	
	H.E........	"Ax"	35	18	—	8	171	176	6	21			435	
4.5"	Howitzers...													
	Shrapnel...	"B"									—	8	8	
	H.E........	"Bx"									15	127	142	

1656

2nd Divisional Artillery Orders

by

Brigadier-General G.H.SANDERS, D.S.O., Comdg.R.A., 2nd Divn.

27th December, 1915.

1212. RETURNS.-CASUALTY

Units are again reminded that they must always report casualties, which occur to Officers, N.C.Os., and Men who are attached for instruction, in their daily casualty return.

1213. TUBE HELMETS.

Os.C.Brigades will submit indents to D.A.D.O.S. at once for Drill Pattern Tube Helmets up to a scale of 29 per Field Artillery Brigade.

1214. COURTMARTIAL.

A F.G.C.M., will assemble at Headquarters, R.A., 2nd Division, (18 RUE SADI-CRANOT, BETHUNE) at 10-0 a.m. on Wednesday, 29th December, 1915, for the trial of No.76939. Dr.H. Swinnerton, 34th B.A.C., and No.34004, Bombardier F.Sullivan, 56th Battery, R.F.A., and such other accused as may be brought before it :-

PRESIDENT.
Major H.H.JOLL,   -   17th Battery, R.F.A.

MEMBERS.
Captain H.E.COURAGE,   -   Divl.Ammn.Column.
Lieuenant H.LOWE,   -   9th Battery, R.F.A.

The accused to be warned and all witnesses **duly** required to attend.
Proceedings to be forwarded to Staff Captain, R.A., 2nd Division.
Court Orderly to be supplied by 44th Brigade, R.F.A.

L.G.BUXTON, Capt, R.A.,
Staff Captain, R.A., 2nd Divn.

Z DIARY

DATE 28-12-15

OBSERVATION CONDITIONS.

WORK DONE BY ENEMY.

MOVEMENT SEEN. Near Lone farm. 2 germans seen walking along trench N.E of Eslainet they then started digging.

GUNS LOCATED OR SUSPECTED.
The hows. firing near Headquarters today are suspected in Vert Feuillage where many men have been seen during recent days.

WORKING PARTIES SEEN.

GENERAL.
There was some shelling in Z2 not reported at 5.30/m in vicinity of signalling lamp in trenches.
On one occasion 16 out of 18 77m did not burst.

ACTION.   See over.

Rodd
Lt. Colonel,
Commanding Z Group.

ACTION Time From	To	Battery	Target	Rounds	Remarks.
9.30 am		9	Lone farm	12	working party dispersed
10.45 am		9	Trenches	35	retaliation
11.45 am		9	Auchy	40	"
1.15 pm		9	Haisnes	50	"
2.15 pm	3 pm	9	Trenches	27	by request
3.45 pm		9	Auchy	30	retaliation
7.45 am		15	Haisnes Lonefarm etc etc	30	registration etc.
10.20 am		15	madagascar t.	11	retaliation
12 noon		15	Trenches	19	retaliation.
1 pm		15	Pekin alley	12	registration
1.15 pm		15	Haisnes	14	retaliation.
3.25	4 pm	15	A28a 0.2	12	Snipers post.
7.50 am		17	Lone farm	3	Working party.
12.25 pm	2.55	17	Haisnes	66	retaliation
			Siding B19C2.6	10	"
			Trenches	92	"
4 pm		17	Trenches	9	"
10.55	11.5 am	47	A28 a 1.3	4	registering snipers post
11.50	11.55 am	47	Haisnes	6	retaliation to 5.9'
2.54 pm	3.30 pm	47	A28a 1.3	52	weekly strong post.
7.30 am	10 am	48	Lone farm & trench	12	
11.30	12 noon	48	registration of zero lines	25	
3.10	4.85	48	Trenches	19	retaliation
3.20	4.15	48	M.G. emplacement	90	weekly strong post.
12.15	1 pm	48	Auchy	29	retaliation.
11.30 am	2.30 p	59	registration	39	by aeroplane
5.30 p		59	Haisnes	15	retaliation.

DIARY

DATE 28/12/15

OBSERVATION CONDITIONS. Wind South slight
Light good. Observation possible
7.15 AM to 4 PM.

WORK DONE BY ENEMY. Enemy have done some new work
repairing CANTELEUX Alley south.
New Earth has been thrown up
at A16 c 9.1. This work is only
just started and it is not yet
possible to say what enemy is building
here

MOVEMENT SEEN. Enemy seen walking along CANTELEUX
ALLEY South at 9 AM.
They were also seen Baling A16 C0.4

GUNS LOCATED OR SUSPECTED. B 7 d 9.7 5.9 Hows firing
on LA BASSÉE road between
CAMBRIN and HARLEY Street.
77 mm Battery firing on
CAMBRIN at 3.30 PM from fuze
and marks was firing from about
HAISNES CEMETERY

WORKING PARTIES SEEN.
9.45 AM By Trucks on RAILWAY line A16 C0.4
12.5 PM NE Brickstack
12.30 PM Two Periscopes seen in front
trench of EMBANKMENT REDOUBT

GENERAL. 12.30 A16 C0.4 Enemy working and baling water

Unfortunately the Divisional relief was
carried out in the morning when 4 of the
enemy's Aeroplanes were up. HARLEY ST
and main LA BASSÉE road were choked
with traffic at the time and The enemy
took advantage of the Target and shelled
CAMBRIN to HARLEY ST with 5.9" Hows
and 77 m m.
The 6" mark VII gun took the opportunity
to fire at the enemy's Balloon which was
up. The flash and smoke of this gun were
clearly visible to the enemy

B Quiller Couch. Lieut & Adj
for Lt. Colonel,
Commanding "A" Group.

ACTION. See over.

ACTION

Time From	Time To	Battery	Target	Rounds	Remarks
9 AM	9.30	71	CANTELEUX	26	Retaliation
9.10 A		56	Railway A	5	"
"		50	NE Brickstack	18	"
9.45 A		50	A 16 c 0 4	7	Working party
10 AM		16	A 22 a 4.7	8	Retaliation
10.15 A	11.40	16	2nd line and support trenches	30	"
10.30	11 AM	71	A 17 a 6.6	20	"
11.15 A		71	CANTELEUX Alley South	30	"
12.5		56	NE Brickstack	7	Working party
12.30		50	Periscopes in Embankment Redoubt	20	
1 PM	1.20	71	TORTOISE	20	Retaliation
2.45	3 PM	50	CANTELEUX ALLEY South	20	Movement seen
"	"	71	TORTOISE	20	Retaliation
3.30 P		16	Enemy's front line	16	"

2nd Divisional Artillery

HOSTILE FIRE REPORT.

28th December, 1915.

1 GENERAL INFORMATION.

Observation possible 7-15 a.m.- 5-50 p.m. With good light.

2 HOSTILE FIRE

No.	Time From	To	Nature	Direction from	Area shelled	Remarks.
1	9-5 a		4.2"	LA BASSEE	KINGSCLERE	
2.	9-15a	9-45a	77 mm.	?	Vicinity G 8 a	15 rds.
3.	10-0a	11-45a	4.2" & 5.9"	LA BASSEE	HARLEY STREET & A 1.	
4.	10-15a		5.9"	?	VERMELLES X Rds.	4 rds.
5.	11-0 a	1-30p	,,	Probably from VERT VEUILL-AGE.	From No.1 HARLEY St. to 19D 14.	? 1 every 2 mins. with 15 minutes interval at 12-45p.
6.	12noon	1-30p		B 7 d 9 7	CAMBRIN	
7.	12-40p	1-15p	5.9"	BEAU PUITS.	LOCK HOUSE ~~POSTOFFICE~~	
8.	12-40p	3-0 p	4.2"	?	PONT FIXE	
9.	3-30p	4-0 p	77 mm.	LA BASSEE	CAMBRIN	
10.	3-15p	4-0p	,,	HAISNES	A 21 b	
11.	3-30p		4.2"	?	19 D.	12 rds.

Capt, R.A.,
Staff Captain, R.A., 2nd Divn.

1658

DAILY AMMUNITION RETURN

DATE 28th Decr. 1915.

BATTERIES.

Piece	Projectile	Code	50	70	15	48	71	9	16	17	47	56	Total Per Piece
18-pr	Guns.......												
	Shrapnel...	"A"	14	14	52	192	30	99	54	5			460
	H. E.......	"Ax"	56	84	3	30	120	41	24	62			420
4.5"	Howitzers..												
	Shrapnel...	"B"									—	—	—
	H. E.......	"Bx"									16	57	73

2nd Divisional Artillery Orders

by

Brigadier-General G.H.SANDERS, D.S.O.,Comdg.R.A.,2nd Division.

28th December,1915.

1215. FIELD CASHIER.

The Field Cashier's Office at 1st Corps Head Quarters will be closed during the mornings from the 28th instant to 5th January,1916.

His Office at BETHUNE will open on Tuesday as usual and on Saturday morning instead of Friday morning.

1216. PROMOTION.

No.65916, Shoeing Smith R.Nicklen is promoted Shoeing Smith Corpl., vice S/S Corporal Eyre, and posted to 34th Brigade, R.F.A., with effect from 28-12-1915.

L.G.BUXTON,Capt, R.A.,

Staff Captain, R.A., 2nd Divn.

Z DIARY

DATE 29-12-15

OBSERVATION CONDITIONS.

Misty in morning. Fair in afternoon.

WORK DONE BY ENEMY.

Infantry report two snipers in advance of german trench A27 b 3.8 and A27 b 45.85.

MOVEMENT SEEN.

GUNS LOCATED OR SUSPECTED.

WORKING PARTIES SEEN.

GENERAL.

The haystack in A28 B was set on fire by our artillery, commencing at 2.40pm.

Communication was established with infantry of 19th Inf. Bde.

ACTION.   See over.

for Roddah
             Lt. Colonel,
        Commanding Z Group.

ACTION

Time From	To	Battery	Target	Rounds	Remarks
8 pm	9 pm	71	Hasines	6	
			Auchy	6	
			Dooth alley	6	
8.45 pm		595	A29a 1.7½	10	
8.50 pm		15	Madagascar t.	17	by request of inf.
6.30 am		15	" "	8	" " "
8.20 am		17	Trenches	6	movement seen
10.15 am		9	Second line t.	12	by request
10.20 am		17	Work	10	in trenches
10.30 am		9	Trenches	12	by request
10.30 am	10.45	48	Trenches	4	retaliation
3.30 pm		9	Hasines Auchy	24	"
3.33 pm		17	Hasines	13	"
3.45 pm		17	"	28	"
4 pm	4.15	48	Trenches	10	"
4.5		17	Germans seen	1	
4.15	4.20	48	Haystack	6	registered for night firing
4.30 pm	4.35	48	Trenches	3	

DIARY

DATE 29/12/15

OBSERVATION CONDITIONS. Wind SE in the morning
to SSW in the afternoon
observation Difficult all day
but possible 7·30 AM to 4 PM.

WORK DONE BY ENEMY. Nothing new to report

MOVEMENT SEEN. 2·30 PM Enemy seen walking
behind trucks A16 d 3.1
3·30 PM About 8 of the enemy seen
moving along road A10 b 9.9 they
stopped and appeared to be laying a
Telephone wire. 2 rounds put them to
GUNS LOCATED OR SUSPECTED. flight.

NIL.

WORKING PARTIES SEEN. 10 AM three men seen working
near false culvert.

GENERAL. The Enemy were very quiet all day
no Artillery fire south of CANAL
except occasional rounds from 77
m.m. on A1 front and 15 minutes shelling
of CAMBRIN by 77 m.m. shrapnel
3·30 PM.

ACTION. See over.

B Quiller Couch
Lieut & Adjt
for
Lt. Colonel,

ACTION Time From	To	Battery	Target	Rounds	Remarks
4.30PM	5 PM	71	CANAL TRENCH	30	Retaliation
5.15PM		16	A 17 c Main Road	10	"
6 PM		71	A17a 6·6 & PLAIN ALLEY	25	"
9.30 PM		71	TORTOISE	25	" for shelling of PONT FIXE

29/12/15

From	To	Battery	Target	Rounds	Remarks
6.15AM		71	CANTELEUX	20	Retaliation
8.55 AM		56	EMBANKMENT	8	Enemy seen working by CULVERT
"		50	"	7	
10.15AM		16	A21 b 9·8	17	Retaliation
11.25AM		56	A BRICKSTACK	14	For Trench Mortar fire
1 PM		"	"	6	"
3.25	3.30PM	16	LA BASSÉE ROAD	28	For shelling of CAMBRIN
3.30	3.45	50	A10 b 9·9	8	Enemy seen on road.

2nd Divisional Artillery

HOSTILE   FIRE   REPORT.

29th December, 1915.

1. GENERAL INFORMATION.

Difficult observation possible 7-15 a.m. to 4-0 p.m. Very quiet day.

2. HOSTILE FIRE.

No.	Time From	Time To	Nature	Direction from	Area shelled.	Remarks.
1.	8-50a	9-0a	77 mm.	?	N. of CANAL.	Trenches 2nd line.
2.	9-30a	10-30a	,,	?	A 21 b	Trenches 40 rds.
3.	10-0a	11-30a	,,	A U C H Y	C M E Trench A 21 a	
4.	12-40p		105 mm.		A 20 d	6 rds.
5.	3-15p	3-25p	77 mm.		Road & CAMBRIN	12 rds.
6.	3-15p	3-30p	,,	A U C H Y	BARRIER	
7.	3-15p	3-45p	,,	HAISNES CEMETERY.	CAMBRIN	

Capt, R.A.,
Staff Captain, R.A., 2nd Divn.

1661

DAILY AMMUNITION RETURN

DATE 29th Decr 1915.

BATTERIES.

Piece	Projectile	Code	50	70	15	48	71	9	16	17	47	56	Total Per Piece
18-pr	Guns.......												
	Shrapnel...	"A"	16	4	74	42	85	113	45	5	—	—	384
	H.E.......	"Ax"	18	85	34	—	29	68	12	216	—	—	462
4.5"	Howitzors..												
	Shrapnel...	"B"										f	
	H.E.......	"Bx"									68	41	109

2nd Divisional Artillery Orders

by

Brigadier-General G.H.SANDERS, D.S.O., Comdg.R.A.,2nd Divn.

29th December,1915.

1217. TUBE HELMETS.

Reference R.A.Order No.1213, dated 27-12-1915.
Units will indent for new Tube Helmets and not "Drill" Tube Helmets as directed in above order. These will replace a similar number of Tube Helmets which have been longest in use which will be marked and used for "drill" purposes.

1218. OFFICERS' SERVANTS.

Under no circumstances whatsoever will any servant be allowed to accompany an individual officer who is leaving France unless the man was that officer's private servant immediately before the War and was specially enlisted to serve with him.
Such cases will be submitted to General Headquarters for approval.

L.G.BUXTON, Capt, R.A.
Staff Captain, R.A.,2nd Divn.

- N O T I C E.-

The R.A.,2nd Divisional Boxing Competition will take place in the Divisional Cinema Theatre at 5-0 p.m. on the evenings of 31st December,1915, and 1st January, 1916.
Details will be circulated by the Hon.Secretary,Lieut. B.B.Quiller Couch, 36th Brigade, to whom all enquiries should be addressed.

Z DIARY

DATE 30-12-15

OBSERVATION CONDITIONS. possible 9.20 am light fair to poor

WORK DONE BY ENEMY.

MOVEMENT SEEN. A searchlight bearing 109° true from 17th Batt position 5.30pm in front of Auchy.

GUNS LOCATED OR SUSPECTED. The guns bearing 112° true from '400' were seen firing from 7.50am to 1pm on the trenches in the vicinity of Hohenzollern.

WORKING PARTIES SEEN. in trenches near "mine point"

GENERAL. The haystack S of Les Briques reported on fire yesterday is still burning.

The haystack (green mound A22d 9.4) North of Les Briques was set on fire today 3.30pm by 59th Siege.

Lamp at DOUVRIN was seen almost immediately after mines went up at 4.28pm.

ACTION. See over.

Rodd
Lt Colonel,
Commanding Z Group.

ACTION

Time From	To	Battery	Target	Rounds	Remarks
9.25a	9.35	9	Trenches	18	retaliation to Minnie
1.15pm	1.30	9	Auchy	20	"
2.15	2.30	9	A22d 8½.4	20	combined shoot with 59th Siege
3 pm	3.10	9	Auchy	10	Retaliation
4 pm	4.13	9	Auchy & Harries	20	"
12.45 pm		15	Madagascar	16	retaliation
2.15 pm		15	"	13	"
2.30 pm		15	"	23	"
7.30 am		17	Germans	3	
1.50 pm		17	Auchy	6	
2.56		17	Trenches	4	
3.45		17	Men in open	2	near tome farm
8 pm	10 pm	48	Auchy alley	9	
9 pm	10 pm	71	Railway tr.	12	
10.40 am		48	Mad alley	8	retaliation
12.35 pm		48	Pekin alley	4	"
1.30 pm	2.30	48	Dook alley	16	"
1.30 pm	2.30	71	Fosse tr.	12	"
2.30	3.30	48	Hindenburg tr. Dook alley	8 29	" "
2.50 pm		48	Auchy	6	"
2 pm		59	A17d 8.7	6	retaliation (Hos. batt)
2.15 pm		59	A22d 9.4	11	rounds in conjunction with 9th Batt 4 hits

DIARY

DATE 30/12/15

OBSERVATION CONDITIONS. Light poor owing to mist. Observation possible 7.15 AM - 4 PM.

WORK DONE BY ENEMY. None seen.

MOVEMENT SEEN.
7.45 AM. Moving along trench A21b
10.35 AM. A17c 1.3 Enemy looking over parapet.

GUNS LOCATED OR SUSPECTED. A6d 3 2 gun flashes and smoke clearly seen on road where guns are hidden in the Houses. They fire on the FESTUBERT Front.

WORKING PARTIES SEEN.
2.20 PM. Enemy digging and baling A22 a 5.8.

GENERAL. Enemy blew a mine opposite Y2 front and shelled the trenches as far north as the LA BASSEE ROAD. Cambrin was shelled as usual about 2.30 PM - 3 PM with 77 m.m.

ACTION. See over.

B Quiller Couch
Lieut & Adjt
for Lt. Colonel,
Commanding A Group

Action Time From	To	Battery	Target	Rounds	Remarks
7.45AM		16	A 21 b	14	Enemy seen.
10.25	11.35	71	A 15 d 7.9 & CANTELEUX	45	Snipers active along CANAL BANK and Retaliation.
10.35		16	A 17 c 1.3	4	
11.15	11.25	56	D & E Brickstack	12	Trench Mortar active
11.20		16	" "	18	" "
11.35		71	A 15 d 7.9	20	Snipers again active
1.15		71	CANAL TRENCH	20	Retaliation
2.20		16	A 22 a 5.8	14	Working Party.
2.45		56	A 6 d 3.2	9	Battery, which stopped firing at once.
2.30	2.55	71	A 17 a & VIOLAINES	40	Retaliation
3.20		56	EMBANKMENT	12	"
3.15	3.45	16	A 21 b 9.5	8	At request of Infantry

2nd Divisional Artillery

HOSTILE FIRE REPORT.

30th December, 1915.

1. GENERAL INFORMATION.

Much shelling commenced at 4-20 p.m., when the Germans blew up two mines. The shelling however was not on "Z" Group front.

2. HOSTILE FIRE.

No.	Time From	Time To	Nature	Direction from	Area shelled	Remarks.
1.	9-15a	9-30a	77 mm.	LA BASSEE	KINGSCLERE	
2.	9-18a	9-25a	,,	AUCHY	CUINCHY	7 rds.
3.	10-20a	10-30a	,,	VIOLAINES	SHADY WALK GIVENCHY	20 rds.
4.	11-20a	11-30a	,,	HAISNES	SPOIL BANK	20 rds.
5.	12-45p	12-50p	,,	AUCHY	Tr.A 27 b	8 rds.
6.	1-10p	3-0p	,,	?	QUEENS ROAD GIVENCHY	80 rds.
7.	1-50p	2-0p	,,	AUCHY	A 21 c A 26 b	12 rds.
8.	1-55p	2-20p	4.2" 77 mm.	HAISNES	SPOIL BANK CANAL TRENCH	
9.	2-10p		77 mm.	LA BASSEE	PONT FIXE	
10.	2-30p	3-30p	,,	AUCHY	A 19 d A 20 c & d	20 rds - some air no damage.
11.	3-20p	3-25p	,,	?	BRIDGE HOUSE HOLLOW	30 rds.
12.	4-0p	5-0p	77 mm. 4.2"	?	A 1 front & 2nd line.	Organised bombardment most noticeable about HOHENZOLLERN & ZO trenches.

Capt, R.A.,
Staff Captain, R.A., 2/Divn.

DAILY AMMUNITION RETURN

DATE 30th Decr 1915.

BATTERIES.

Piece	Projectile	Code	50	70	15	48	71	9	16	17	47	56	Total	Per Piece
18-pr	Guns.......													
	Shrapnel...	"A"	16	10	-	44	34	12	69	7	—		192	
	H. E.......	"Ax"	6	78	-	10	53	32	8	18	—		205	
4.5"	Howitzers..													
	Shrapnel...	"B"												
	H. E.......	"Bx"									8	20	28	

2nd Divisional Artillery Orders

by

Brigadier-General G.H.SANDERS, D.S.O., Comdg.R.A.,2nd Divn.

30th December,1915.

1219. COMMISSIONS.

Os.C.Brigades will send in a list by 8-0 p.m. on 1st January,1916, of all Temporary and Special Reserve Officers who received their commissions between 5th August 1914, and 31st December 1914.

1220. COURTMARTIAL.

A F.G.C.M., will assemble at Headquarters, R.A., 2nd Division, (18 RUE SADI-CARNOT,BETHUNE) at 10-0 a.m. on Monday 3rd January, 1916, for the trial of No.75279,Dr. E.S.Whitmarch 2nd D.A.C.; No.57033, Dr. William Trought, 2nd D.A.C.; No. 57149, Br. James Jackson, 2nd D.A.C.; No.17740, Br.J.T.Prosser, 2nd D.A.C., and such other accused as may be brought before it

PRESIDENT.
Major W.A.F.JONES.   -   70th Battery, R.F.A.

MEMBERS.
Captain V.WALROND.   -   71st Battery, R.F.A.
2nd Lieut.C.H.N.YOUNG.   -   9th Battery, R.F.A.

The accused to be warned and all witnesses duly required to attend.
Proceedings to be forwarded to Staff Captain, R.A., 2nd Division.
Court Orderly to be supplied by 2nd D.A.C.

1221. ORDERLIES.

Os.C.Units will please give orders to N.C.Os. and men who are sent to this office for any purpose that they are not to go away until they have seen an officer or received a letter or some written message.

L.G.BUXTON,Capt,R.A.,
Staff Captain, R.A., 2/Divn.

Z group DIARY

DATE 31-12-15

1666

OBSERVATION CONDITIONS. Fair till 3 pm.

WORK DONE BY ENEMY. More work on PEKIN Tr. has been done and fresh wire put up. There seems to be a light railway in front of Pekin tr. 2 rails and 3 trolleys visible.

MOVEMENT SEEN. A party at 8 am in A22 b 85.75 mending telephone wires two men.
At 10.45 am a party of about 15 men emerged from a hole near the burning haystack A22 d 8.4 (or near) and disappeared among the houses A22 a 9.6.

GUNS LOCATED OR SUSPECTED.

WORKING PARTIES SEEN. — near Pekin trench as above.
— in A22 d 8.5
— just N. Lone Farm
— MINE point.

GENERAL. Quite a lot of hostile shelling today.
59th Siege fired on house at A10 d 10.9. No hits on house were obtained but dug out along side was much damaged. The telephone wires to dug out were cut. During each interval of fire several germans were seen outside the dug out and were fired on by 70b Battery. As many as 12 were seen. Their uniforms seemed quite clean. The house A10 d 10.9 was also damaged.
The haystack A22 d 7.4 is still burning.

Rudolphs
Adj   Lt. Colonel,
                   Commanding Z Group.

ACTION.   See over.

ACTION Time From	To	Battery	Target	Rounds	Remarks
7.45	7.55	9	A23d 6.9	10	
8 am	8.5		A22 b 88	16	
11 am	11.15		Trenches	24	by request
11.30	11.48		A23d 2.2	30	suspected O.B. Instruction
2 pm	2.10		Trenches	20	by request
2.30	2.50		Second line	15	suspected O.B. "
3.30	3.45		A22d 8.5	10	working party
3.45	3.50		Lone farm	8	"
8 am		15	Com trenches	5	by request
11.15 am			Madagascar tr	15	"
12.30 pm			" "	15	"
11.37		17	trenches	7	retaliation
2.7 pm			"	9	"
2.45 pm			"	9	"
4 pm			"	6	working party
11.3	12.5	47	Ryaws heep	4	retaliation
7 pm	9 pm	48	M.G. near 'popes nose'	24	
11.30 pm	11.45	48	" "	4	
10.45	11 am	48	Trenches	10	retaliation
12 noon	12.15		"	20	"
2 pm	2.5		"	10	
2.30	2.40		Auchy	10	registration
11 am		59	A10d 10.9	77	demolition
2 pm			A17d 8.9	15	by aeroplane. (Host. Batt)
			Haystack SE Cantelleux	21	demolition

No 1.

DIARY A. Group.

DATE 31. 12. 15.

OBSERVATION CONDITIONS.
Observation possible at 7.15 a.m. a good light.

WORK DONE BY ENEMY.
Working parties seen at Embankment Redoubt and near NE BRICKSTACK.

MOVEMENT SEEN.
Germans in open at CANTELEUX. Standing telephone wires destroyed by shelling of house at A.10.d.9.9. (This was destroyed)

GUNS LOCATED OR SUSPECTED.
✓

WORKING PARTIES SEEN.
✓

GENERAL.
Between 12.45 and 1 pm, about 2 pm and again at between 3.15 pm and 3.45 pm PONT FIXE HOLLOW and CUINCHY were heavily shelled by 77 MM and 105 MM & 10 CM Naval Gun. The infantry reported the 105 MM as gas shells. The Survey Officers reported them as the new H.E. being used by the Germans which gives off a considerable amount of white smoke similar to the earlier

ACTION. See over.   Lt.Colonel,
                                     Commanding

ACTION Time From	To	Battery	Target	Rounds	Remarks
A.M.					
8.10		50th	Working party Embankment Redoubt.	3	
10. a.m.		56th	Working party near N.E. BRICK STACK	16	
11.30		"	"	2	
10.30		71st	Snipers post on Embankment	20	
11.30		16th	LA BASSEE Rd	3	in Retaliation
11.30		71st	CANTELEUX	27	In Retaliation
11.45		16th	LA BASSEE Rd	5	" "
12.34		56th	CANAL HOUSE & TORTOISE	19	Retaliation
12.15		71st	CANTELEUX	24	"
12.50 1.50 2.45		50th	Germans in open seen. Some dislodged by 6" How. Appears to be unusually heavy shelling.		
1 p.m.		71st	PLAIN ALLEY and SUPPORT TRENCHES	21	In Retaliation
1.30		56th	"DUG OUT" at CANTELEUX	12	Germans seen in the open here.

3.

ACTION Time		Battery	Target	Rounds	Remarks
From	To				
3.30		56th	Trench in A2.	16	At request of Infantry in retaliation
3.45		56th	CANAL TRENCH	4	In retaliation to shelling of the Hohen.
3.50		50th	EMBANKMENT REDOUBT.	20	In retaliation.

DIARY

DATE
_____

OBSERVATION CONDITIONS.

WORK DONE BY ENEMY.

MOVEMENT SEEN.

GUNS LOCATED OR SUSPECTED.

WORKING PARTIES SEEN.

GENERAL.

ACTION.   See over.   Lt.Colonel,
                                         Commanding

DIARY

DATE
_____

OBSERVATION CONDITIONS.

WORK DONE BY ENEMY.

MOVEMENT SEEN.

GUNS LOCATED OR SUSPECTED.

WORKING PARTIES SEEN.

(Continued)

GENERAL.

Shells down in use by us.
The lorrie at A.10.d.9.9. was destroyed
by the 59th Seige and Germans in
the open were seen subsequently
mending telephone wires and were
fired at. Infantry also
reported Gas Bombs on A, subsection.

H. Ward.

ACTION.   See over.   Lt.Colonel,
                                        Commanding

2/

ACTION Time		Battery	Target	Rounds	Remarks
From	To				
1.30		16th	Working Party A.21.b.8.6.	10	
2.0		16th	Front and Support trenches	16	In Retaliation.
2.15		16th	Support Trenches in A.21.b	8	At request of Infantry in Retaliation.
2.20		16th	Front line Trenches	23	In Retaliation.
2.30		56th	Support Trenches in A₂	16	In Retaliation at request of Infantry.
2.55		56th	EMBANKMENT REDOUBT	31	In retaliation & heavy shelling of PONT FIXE & CHEYNE WALK.
3.pm		50th	EMBANKMENT REDOUBT	25	In Retaliation.
3.pm		71st	PLAIN ALLEY & Support Trenches	25	At request of Infantry.
3.15		50th	EMBANKMENT REDOUBT & trenches in A₂	80	In Retaliation.
3.pm		16th	Front trench in A1.	3	In Retaliation.
3.20		16th	" "	7	" "
3.30		16th	" "	6	In retaliation for bombing at request of Infantry.

2nd Divisional Artillery

HOSTILE FIRE REPORT.

31st Decr., 1915.

1. GENERAL INFORMATION.

About 12-45 p.m. and again at 3-20 p.m. there was a considerable amount of hostile shelling. 77 mm. & 105 mm. Observing officers did not think the shells were gas shells but only the new explosive used in the 105 mm. which gives a quantity of white smoke, rather similar to our AMATOL.

2. HOSTILE FIRE.

No.	Time From	Time To	Nature	Direction from	Area shelled.	Remarks.
1.	9-0a		77 mm.	Rly.TRIANGLE.	Trenches.	12 Rds.
2.	11-15a	11-30a	,,	A U C H Y	Com.Trenches in A 2.	A few rounds.
3.	11-20a		,,	LA BASSEE	Rd in A 21 a	(2 Salvoes of 3 (rounds.
4.	11-35a		,,	?	A 21 d 5 2	4 rds.
5.	11-40a		,,	LA BASSEE	Rd in A 21 a	(2 Salvoes of (3 rounds.
6.	12-15p	12-30p	10 cm.	LA BASSEE	PONT FIXE	A few rounds.
7.	12-45p	1-0p	,,	?	HOLLOW & Com.Trenches in A2.	)) 40 to 50) Rounds.
8.	12-55p	1-0p	77 mm.	A U C H Y	PONT FIXE.	)
9.	1-55p	2-15p	105 mm.	,,	Support Trenches in A 21a & 7	1 round per 3 minutes.
10.	1-55p	2-15p	77 mm.	Rly.TRIANGLE	(BURBURE	
11.	2-30p	2-45p		,,	(MAISON ROUGE (RIDGE.	
12.	2-0p	2-10p	77 mm.	A U C H Y(?)	LA BASSEE Road.	1 rd.per 30 secs. (15 rounds).
13.	2-10p		105 mm.	?	STAFFORD REDOUBT	20 rds. (reported by Infy.as gas shells).
14.	2-15p		,,	A U C H Y	Support Trenches in A 21 a	20 rounds.
15.	2-55p	3-11p	,,	?	STAFFORD REDOUBT	1 rd.per 2 mins.
16.	3-0p		,,	HAISNES	Trenches.	8 rounds.
17.	3-15p	3-30p	,,	?	STAFFORD REDOUBT	6 rds.
18.	3-25p		Gas Bomb (?).		Front Line.	Reported by Infantry.
19.	3-25p	3-40p	105 mm.	?	PONT FIXE Trenches in A2. HOLLOW CUINCHY & HUN VIEW	
20.	3-25p	3-40p	77 mm.	A U C H Y	Trenches in B1.	
21.	3-45p	3-50p	105 mm.	?	ORCHARD ROAD.	
Also.-						
22.	2-25p	2-50p	105 mm.		CUINCHY	
23.	2-25p	2-50p	77 mm.		Trenches in A1 & A2.	

Capt, R.A.,
Staff Captain, R.A., 2/Divn.

1667

DAILY AMMUNITION RETURN

DATE 31st Dec 1915.

BATTERIES.

Piece	Projectile	Code	50	70	15	48	71	9	16	17	47	56	Total Per Piece
18-pr	Guns.......												
	Shrapnel...	"A"	42	60	70	41	39	72	27	7			358
	H. E.......	"Ax"	65	222	9	66	98	83	9	11			563
4.5"	Howitzers..												
	Shrapnel...	"B"									—	—	
	H. E.......	"Bx"									—	77	77

www.ingramcontent.com/pod-product-compliance
Lightning Source LLC
Chambersburg PA
CBHW080912230426
43667CB00015B/2659